D1320820

Our
Place
in
the
Cosmos

WEST GRID STAMP

NN		RR	7/53	WW	
NT		RT		WO	
NC		RC		WL	
NH		RB		WM	
NL		RP		WT	
NV		RS		WA	
NM		RW		WR	
NB		RV		WG	
NE					
NP					

Our
Place
in
the
Cosmos

THE UNFINISHED REVOLUTION

FRED HOYLE

AND

CHANDRA WICKRAMASINGHE

J M Dent London

To Daisaku Ikeda

Typeset by Selwood Systems,
Midsomer Norton

Made and printed in Great Britain by
Butler & Tanner Ltd, Frome and London

J M Dent Ltd
The Orion Publishing Group
Orion House
5 Upper St Martin's Lane
London WC2H 9EA

A catalogue record for this book is available from the British Library

ISBN: 0 460 86084 4

CONTENTS

FIGURES

You should live as lamps unto yourselves. Hold fast to the lamp of Truth. Take refuge only in Truth. Look not to refuge to anyone beside yourself . . .

Gautama Buddha
(sixth century BC)

PROLOGUE

The popular belief is that the Copernican Revolution and the inquisition of Galileo are things of the past. Human societies, it is claimed, have progressed beyond the stage when such outrages could happen again. In this book we show that the Copernican Revolution is far from over, and that society has not improved since the sixteenth century in any important respect. If anything the situation may have got worse, with the successes of the Industrial Revolution conferring upon human beings a degree of arrogance not seen before. The dogma has shifted from an Earth-centred Universe to the equally unlikely idea that life, which is the most complex and amazingly intricate phenomenon in the entire cosmos, must be centred on the Earth. The new dogma has Judeo-Christian roots, but today its custodians are scientists rather than the high priests of the Church.

Our capacity to probe the Universe around us, to ask and discuss questions concerning origins (always to ask, sometimes to answer), sets us apart from all other creatures that inhabit our planet. This remarkable capacity, or intelligence as we prefer to call it, may be seen as the end product of a long history, a history that according to the thesis of this book must have predated the formation of the Earth some 4500 million years ago. For close upon 4000 million years, terrestrial life meandered along in a seemingly mindless way. Starting from microscopic single-celled creatures, it built up to become more and more complex, more and more sophisticated and diverse, through long periods of geological time, until at last a species emerged that was endowed with the capacity to look back on the very processes that created it. We are all members of that uniquely privileged species.

How did this whole process come about? Did it arise through a sequence of random events here on the Earth, or was it instigated from outside the Earth, from space, and is it even possible that it might have been driven by the agency of an external cosmic intelligence? These are some of the questions we shall address in later chapters of this book.

The orthodox explanation of these facts, which is attributed to Charles Darwin and a long succession of his disciples, is well known. In its modern extended form, Darwinian theory asserts that the earliest living cell was assembled through a purely mechanistic shuffling of the basic building blocks of life, and that subsequent mistakes of copying (mutations) and occasional doublings of genes, together with a continual sieving out of the 'unfit' in relation to every terrestrial environment, led to the products of evolution that are seen today. All this is taught nowadays as though it embodied proven unquestionable facts, but in reality it is little more than dogma, dogma that has come to be fossilized in our educational system. A great deal of this dogma has turned out in recent years to be inconsistent with the real world. Yet the theory dies hard. This unfortunate situation has arisen through a sustained campaign of propaganda on the part of biologists, and by a blind eye being turned to every fact to emerge in later years that appeared to go against the theory. Several distinguished physicists have questioned the basic premises of this essentially pre-Copernican, earthbound theory and attempted to point the way towards a cosmic view of life. Among them are figures of no less stature than Kelvin, Helmholtz and Arrhenius, but all their protestations have come to naught in the face of the unrelenting propaganda of the Darwinian front. In addition to the conflict with Darwinism, the idea of terrestrial life being influenced by the external Universe runs counter to a long-established belief in the Christian Church. By about the sixth century AD, Christian beliefs included the dogma that nothing that happens in the heavens could have any conceivable effect on the Earth. The heavens were merely an adornment that was of no practical importance in day-to-day life (except for the Sun, whose beneficial effects were not denied).

We begin our book by recounting the beginning of the Copernican Revolution, in the fifteenth and sixteenth centuries, which still appears to have repercussions to the present day. Next we discuss the sociological forces that operated effectively to raise Darwin's theory from the reasonable speculation that it was: first to belief, then to entrenched dogma, and finally to the exalted status of 'irrefutable fact'. The situation that now faces us is potentially dangerous, not merely for a handful of interested scientists but for the entire human species. For when human beings collectively refuse to distinguish propositions about the world that are demonstrably true from those that are manifestly false, we must surely be heading down a road to disaster. The struggle against the power of the Church in the 1860s that fuelled Darwinian propaganda in the early years might now, in the 1990s, be transformed into a blueprint for ultimate extinction.

In this book we present evidence, which we think is irrefutable, to support our point of view that life is a cosmic phenomenon. At the same time we seek to analyse the sociological forces that appear to be rallied against an acceptance of this point of view. Components of cosmic life were, in our view, added to our planet in the form of bacteria and viruses from space, and perhaps, in a remarkable event which occurred about 570 million years ago, whole creatures arrived here from space; it has been from this cosmic assembly that terrestrial life has evolved over long periods of geological time. The rival theory asserts, without any tangible proof or evidence, that electric discharges in the atmosphere of a primitive Earth led to the inception of terrestrial life. The only empirical basis that could conceivably be claimed for this assertion is that the chemical building blocks of life – amino acids, nucleotides, sugars – have been synthesized under laboratory conditions that were considered to mimic conditions that may have existed on a primitive Earth. It has also been shown experimentally that these molecular units could be made to form into long polymer chains resembling, very superficially, biological polymers. Yet the result of such experiments is a far cry from life itself. All such experiments and inferences beg the most important question of all: the origin of the information content of life. The information content of life (that is to say, the information needed to put life together) is specific in kind, and super-astronomical in quantity. How was this highly specific information acquired in the first place, out of initial chaos? Darwin's allegorical 'warm little pond', cosy as it may sound, will scarcely suffice.

Astronomical evidence accumulated over the past decade has pointed to the existence of vast quantities of complex organic molecules in interstellar space. Moreover, we ourselves have found that the observed properties of cosmic dust grains are similar to the properties of freeze-dried bacteria as measured in the laboratory. The correspondences between our model and the data are so precise that we have been encouraged to suggest that cosmic dust grains are indeed bacteria, implying that cosmic microbiology operates and evolves on a galactic scale.

It is a necessary corollary to this point of view that bacteria must be space-hardy, and so indeed they are found to be. For example, a viable strain of *Streptococcus mitis* was recovered after two years of exposure to conditions on the surface of the Moon. It has been shown that bacteria can be taken down to near zero pressure and temperature without loss of viability, provided suitable care is exercised in the experimental conditions. Bacteria can survive after exposure to pressures as high as 10 tonnes per square centimetre, and after flash heating under dry conditions at temperatures of up to 600°C. Viable bacteria have been recovered from the interior of an operating nuclear reactor, having survived intense fluxes of ionizing radiation. These are not properties one would expect to have evolved on the Earth, but they are all properties necessary for survival in space.

At the birth of the Solar System, cometary bodies condensed at about the distances of the present planets Uranus and Neptune. We argue that even the smallest population of cosmic bacteria present within this primordial comet cloud would have been vastly amplified within individual comets in their warm watery interiors on a very short timescale.

4

Biological material from a comet is peeled away layer by layer when it approaches the inner regions of the Solar System. Some of this material could rain down intact onto the surfaces of the planets, including the Earth, providing the genetic building blocks from which life evolved. The recent return of Comet Halley offered a unique opportunity to test this theory of comets. We had predicted that the surface of the comet would at close quarters look dark, like an organic tarry substance, and so it was found to be. We also argued that a spectral signature of bacteria and viruses would be seen in the cometary dust, and this prediction was also verified to a startling degree of accuracy. We also predicted that the proportions of the chemical elements in the dust would be like those in bacteria, and sure enough they were.

Upwards of 10^{11} (1 followed by 11 zeros, or 100 billion) life-bearing comets, in our view, envelop the Solar System, populating the so-called Oort cometary cloud. From time to time, individual comets are deflected out of this cloud into the inner regions of the Solar System by interaction with a passing star or molecular cloud. At the present time we know that only a few cometary objects each year are thus deflected to show up as new comets, but in the past much larger numbers might have been deflected, and cometary incursions would then have been much more frequent.

A life-bearing comet arriving at an Earth that had already acquired its oceans and atmosphere would effectively have seeded our planet with life. From the available geological evidence it would seem that this first successful seeding occurred about 3800 million years ago. However, the process of cometary injection of life could not have stopped at this distant prehistoric time. Comets are with us in the Solar System today, and the Earth continually picks up debris from comets. About 1000 tonnes of cometary debris enter the Earth's atmosphere every year, a fraction of which must surely contain micro-organisms that actually arrive at the Earth's surface in a viable state.

This conclusion, bold though it may be, has the advantage of being susceptible to testing, especially if the Earth is being showered with microorganisms that are pathogenic to plants and animals. Viral and bacterial invasions could thus lead to epidemic outbreaks of, for example, influenza. The known patterns of influenza outbreaks over the surface of the Earth clearly prove, in our view, the direct incidence of the causative pathogen from space. This conclusion seems to have been reached by medieval doctors and readily conceded well into the nineteenth century. But nowadays the facts that relate to these matters are often suppressed or distorted by a society eager to disown its cosmic heritage.

Besides influenza, a wide range of other viral and bacterial diseases are also caused by the introduction of causative agents from outside the Earth. Many common epidemic diseases have a record of abrupt entrances, exits and re-entrances – exactly as though the Earth were being seeded at periodic intervals. In the case of smallpox, the time interval between successive entrances appears to have been about 700–800 years. Likewise, periodic occurrences of bubonic plague in historical times, and of epidemics such as the plague of Athens, all point to a direct incidence from space. In recent times, it would seem that the 3.5-year period of whooping cough can best be linked to bacteria expelled from Comet Encke. We also argue that highly localized outbreaks of viral and bacterial diseases (e.g. legionnaire's disease, viral meningitis) can be interpreted as the effect of small cometary bodies that enter the atmosphere and become dispersed near ground level over local areas of the Earth's surface.

To sum up: we argue that a wide range of facts point decisively to life being a phenomenon that must be connected with the much wider cosmos outside the Earth. Life on Earth is derived from an all-pervasive, galaxy-wide biological system. Life was derived from and continues to be driven by sources outside the Earth, in direct contradiction to neo-Darwinian theory as it is generally understood. Our theory of biology has applications that are of immediate practical importance, for instance in the prevention or alleviation of the ravages of future epidemic disease. It would appear that there lies ahead a sociological struggle to get human beings to respect objective truth, even when such truth runs counter to prevailing beliefs. The very survival of our species could well be at stake.

CHAPTER ONE

On the tendency of human societies to depart indefinitely from the objective truth

We are all in a mysterious situation, born as we are into a strange world without anyone troubling themselves even to ask our permission. We learn in our earliest months, with an amazing precociousness; first to see, then to stand and talk. Eventually we burst through the language barrier, understanding what others are saying, and speaking ourselves, without having any previous knowledge of language in our minds to serve as an example. We learn all these things seemingly out of nowhere. The one unfortunate thing, however, is that at this stage we have no really effective way of telling the adults around us the unvarnished truth about the state of the world, so they are permitted to go on living with illusions – illusions of which they would soon be disabused were a proper two-way system of communication available. The sad thing is that, by the time we acquire the ability to com-municate such unprejudiced views, we have lost them because of the process of education.

Education does of course have a good side to it: it gives easy access to a thousand and one items of indisputably correct knowledge, ranging from the abstract processes of mathematics to the correct way to make a horse's collar (a good horse's collar being one that gets more work from the horse than the choke used by the civilizations of Greece and Rome). Education ensures that knowledge which is factual and correct carries forward from one generation to the next, and because of the forward momentum of this process technology too moves unerringly forward. Trouble comes, however, when what we think to be knowledge is actually no more than illusion. Education then serves to transmit illusions from generation to generation, with the situation getting worse all the time. A mild illusion in one generation becomes less mild in the next, each generation impressing on its successors a growing belief in the illusion. As a mathematician might put it, the educational system is unstable against the spread of incorrect beliefs; wrong ideas eventually become so deeply entrenched as to become unshakeable dogma. This is basically why, sooner or later, all nations and all cultures go into decline: the burden of dogma builds up more and more until its weight causes the social structures to collapse.

The situation in this respect is worse today than it ever was in the past, because the educational process at higher levels nowadays continues to the age of about twenty-five, the age at which advanced students complete the requirements for the Ph.D. degree. By this time it is too late to return to the inner inventiveness of childhood, far too late to put right mistakes in the system, far too late to escape from the mental prison-houses in which as students we have been locked up for so long.

In the nineteenth century it was less difficult for boys leaving school at fourteen or even earlier to make an immense mark on the world. George Stephenson was able to laugh almost audibly at a parliamentary committee of 'experts' who declared that his project for building a railway from Manchester to Liverpool was an impossibility. Evidence was given at great length showing the utter impossibility of forming a road of any kind over Chat Moss, an exceedingly swampy terrain. Mr Francis Giles, the Chief Engineer, had been 22 years in the profession and could speak with some authority:

No Engineer in his senses would go through that moss if he wanted to make a railroad from Liverpool to Manchester. In my judgement a rail road certainly cannot be safely made over that moss without going to the bottom of the Moss. The soil ought all to be taken out, undoubtedly; in doing which, it will not be practicable to approach each end of the cutting, as you make it, with the carriages. No carriages would stand upon the Moss short of the bottom. My estimate for the whole cutting and embankment over Chat Moss is £270,000, nearly, at those quantities and those prices which are decidedly correct. It will be necessary to take this Moss completely out at the bottom, in order to make a solid road. (Samuel Smiles, *The Lives of Engineers*, David & Charles, 1968).

Can one imagine a government committee today rejecting such advice from an expert witness in favour of the contrary opinion of a man who, like George Stephenson, had no schooling at all? Can one even imagine a Ph.D. student standing up to his professor over the professor's opinion that it was necessary 'to take this Moss completely out at the bottom'? Yet as it turned out:

The road across Chat Moss was finished by 1st January 1830, where the first experimental train of passengers passed over it, drawn by the 'Rocket', and it turned out that, instead of being the most expensive part of the line, it was about the cheapest. The total cost of forming the line over the Moss was £28,000, not the 'decidedly correct' estimate of £270,000. It also proved to be one of the best portions of the railway. Being a floating road, it was smooth and easy to run upon.... There was, and still is, a sort of springiness in the road over the Moss. (*Ibid.*)

The invention of the horse's collar in the West, around AD 700, an invention that had entirely escaped the formidable civilizations of Greece and Rome, doubtless came from some young fellow who, like George Stephenson, had not attended school at all. All this, one might be tempted to say, is ancient history and not relevant to the present day. While it is generally acknowledged that in past times the world suffered from monstrous illusions, the present-day belief is that, by being educated for longer and longer, we have somehow been freed from illusion; in fact the opposite is much more likely to be true, for the longer one is immersed in a wrong situation the more self-deceiving it could become.

It is not hard to identify the kind of problems and situations where illusions are likely today to be most deeply rooted. Wherever ultimate origins are concerned, one finds, not the caution and humility that common sense might suggest to be advisable, but an immense show of intellectual arrogance. Almost every week nowadays one reads that the Universe originated in a Big Bang, not *might* have originated that way, but *did* originate that way, undoubtedly. A detailed picture is developed of how all the matter in the Universe was compressed essentially into a point source that 'exploded' at some definite moment in the past. The truth is that we have no such knowledge. All one can properly say is that, if there was a Big Bang of a certain kind, then there would be consequences which happen to match one particular observed aspect of the world relating to the abundances of the so-called light elements – which it is also possible to explain otherwise. Two other aspects have also been counted as successes by Big Bang advocates, but one of them can also be explained otherwise rather easily, while the other (the cosmic microwave background) has very recently been found to have properties that seem likely to prove an embarrassment to the Big Bang. This is not much for a belief to develop around, but develop it has, to a point where there is no shortage today of half-informed commentators who assure their readers that it is really and irrefutably so.

There is nothing wrong in trying to understand ultimate questions, provided one realizes from the beginning that such an aim is a bit like trying to steal apples. Make the attempt if you like, but do not be surprised if you get caught. One of the present writers was involved in the first work on what nowadays would be called an inflationary cosmology. The title of his paper, 'A new model for the expanding Universe', meant just what it said: a new idea available for discussion, not a final decisive answer to what is plainly the most immense of all scientific problems. The essential point of this paper of 1948, namely a connection between the creation of matter and the expansion of the Universe via a new concept of negative pressure, survives to this day, although the astronomical framework into which the discussion was fitted is nowadays changed. This is pretty much the best one can hope for in trying to steal apples – a partial survival of the original plan.

A river flows smoothly over a near-horizontal bed. Suddenly, however, the bed of the river falls a few metres – a common enough occurrence. Describing the initial smooth flow mathematically is fairly easy, but anything like a full description of all the physical phenomena set in train by the sudden drop of the river bed, especially if the drop itself has irregularities in it, would be ferociously hard, harder than any mathematics yet used to describe the origin of the Universe. Now, quite clearly the whole Universe is not going to be simpler than the flow of water in almost any stream or river, so it is evident that we make simplistic attempts to understand the Universe at our peril. This is not to debar such attempts; rather, like a surgeon attempting a difficult operation, we must know exactly what we are doing.

Some parts of present-day knowledge are clear-cut. No matter how much science may advance in the future, no matter how complex the Universe turns out to be, what we clearly know to be true cannot become untrue. The essence of knowing what you are doing lies in being aware to a hair's breadth of the distinction between such certain knowledge and mere conventional opinion and dogma. Opinion and dogma can be booted out of the window, if you please, but certain knowledge must be respected to its last letter, number and symbol. It is just here that the educational system makes things so difficult for the student. By being rushed from one examination to another at breakneck speed (as in the tripos system at Cambridge, to take what is perhaps the most extreme example), there is no time for the brain to order its priorities correctly. In respect of what really matters in the learning process, it can be said with some emphasis that it does not pay to be a student for too long.

The trap operates both ways. Just as, within the educational system, dogma becomes easily confused with knowledge, so from the outside it is all too easy not to respect, or even to understand, the certain areas of knowledge. Certain knowledge is not something one can take or leave as one pleases. It has to be taken, and if it happens to be medicinal in taste, then one must swallow it without complaint. The books of Immanuel Velikovsky (*Worlds in Collision, Ages in Chaos* and *Earth in Upheaval*) caused a sensation both with the public and among scientists when they first appeared about thirty years ago. What was unexpected was Velikovsky's total rejection of a certain area of knowledge, knowledge attested to by tens of thousands of facts derived from observation and experiment. Velikovsky lived in Princeton, New Jersey, and he often attended astronomy seminars held at the observatory of Princeton University, where one of the present authors met him on a number of occasions. He seemed to believe quite genuinely that the contents of ancient documents were of greater reliability than the science of celestial mechanics, which is one of the best understood and closely studied parts of science. This wrong judgement was probably due in considerable measure to the natural bias we all have in favour of what we happen to know well. Velikovsky had an expert understanding of ancient languages, so he could translate the documents in which he put his trust, whereas his knowledge of the precision mathematics of celestial mechanics was virtually nil. This is a good example of how one may and may not attempt to steal apples. Stealing apples means rejecting a dogmatic component of the beliefs of experts. But before making a raid on the orchard you have to master the details of the expert view in the certain areas of knowledge. Otherwise you will surely be caught.

Velikovsky was caught, in the public eye, not by the fury of contemporary scientists, but by the development of the space programme. Space probes can be set on courses that are predicted even years ahead to reach precisely specified targets, as for example in the recent Giotto encounters with Comet Halley and Comet Grigg–Skjellerup, in which the probe was set on a path to within an accuracy of ten kilometres or so. If Velikovsky had been right in his dismissal of celestial mechanics, that error would have been something like 100 million kilometres. The public can now see that when scientists calculate from celestial mechanics they are vindicated, which every mathematically oriented scientist has known for generations to be true because celestial mechanics is an area of certain knowledge, an area that within its stated measure of accuracy is never going to be changed, however much science progresses in centuries to come. The same cannot be said for the latest sophisticated theory in particle physics or the latest theory of the origin of the Universe, both of which are subject to change without notice. In stealing apples you have to know exactly the difference between the strong and weak points in the position of conformist opinion and dogma. In other words, you have to know exactly where the owners of the orchard have set their traps.

Let us pass from Velikovsky to the targets of modern scientific fury, 'creationism' and 'creationists'. The meanings presently attached to these words are unfortunate degradations of language. On the verb 'to create' the *Concise Oxford Dictionary* says: 'bring into existence . . . make or cause . . . originate (*an actor creates a part*) . . . invest (a person) with rank . . . make a fuss, grumble'. And on the noun 'creation': 'the act of creating . . . the creating of the universe regarded as an act of God . . . a product of human intelligence, esp. of imaginative thought or artistic ability . . . the act of investing with a title or rank'. But when we come to the noun 'creationism', we run into something quite different: 'a theory attributing all matter, biological species, etc. to separate acts of creation, rather than to evolution'.

The odd thing about modern scientific dogma is that to be respectable you must be a half-believer in creationism. You must believe matter to have arisen in a Big-Bang Universe by special creation, but you must not believe that biological species arose by special creation. Those who believe both are considered beyond the pale, as are those – like ourselves – who believe neither. Where 'creationism' is concerned you have to get it just right: one half one way, the other half the other way, otherwise the editors of scientific journals will force you to walk the plank, and those who disburse public money on science will laugh you to scorn.

An even more remarkable transmogrification occurs when '-ist' is added to 'creation', a transmogrification from an actor creating a part to a believer in the literal interpretation of the biblical Pentateuch, a believer particularly in the Book of Genesis. How difficult the English language has become! The writer(s) of the Book of Genesis were equipped with scarcely any scientific knowledge as we understand it today, so their description of cosmology was inevitably primitive, a crude interpretation with which the creationist is nowadays encumbered. Chronology is a matter of especial embarrassment, for according to the Book of Genesis the earth has existed for hardly a tick of the cosmic clock, only a few thousand years.

On every day of the year, visitors make their way to High Force, a waterfall near Middleton-in-Teesdale in Durham, England. This particular waterfall has special interest because there the river Tees is cutting its way back into a flattish sheet of extremely hard rock called the Whin Sill. The rate of cutting can hardly be more than a few centimetres per century; even very simple observations made over a fraction of a lifetime would show that the rate cannot be more than about 30 centimetres per century. Yet the gorge and V-shaped valley below the present-day waterfall are together over a kilometre long. Since this valley has clearly been cut by the river in times gone by, the time required for the cutting must have been at least a few thousand centuries, requiring the Earth to have had a long past history. Similar situations can be found in many places.

The creationist is a sham religious person who, curiously, has no true sense of religion. In the language of religion, it is the facts we observe in the world around us that must be seen to constitute the words of God. Documents, whether the Bible, the Quoran or those writings that held such force for Velikovsky, are only the words of men. To prefer the words of men to those of God is what one can mean by blasphemy. This we think is the instinctive point of view of most scientists who, curiously again, have a deeper understanding of the real nature of religion than have the many who delude themselves into a frenzied belief in the words, often the meaningless words, of men. Indeed, the lesser the meaning, the greater the frenzy, in something like inverse proportion.

By 'science', in the previous paragraph, we mean areas of certain knowledge. When one passes from certain knowledge to still unsolved problems the situation becomes different; conformist opinion and dogma then take over. 'Scientists' often cease to be real scientists, preferring dogma to facts, thereby adopting the same mental processes as the creationists. This was the essence of the testimony given by one of us in defence of the state of Arkansas in 1981. The state was under trial before a US Federal Court on account of an educational policy that permitted a hearing to the creationists, who form a fair fraction of the population in that region of the United States and whose taxes help support the education system. The whole affair struck us as an odd phenomenon in a land that was supposed to be dedicated to the concept of free speech. Our point of view was that in their interpretation of the origin and development of life on the Earth, the so-called evolutionists were just as surely wrong as the creationists, but whereas it is easy to see that the creationists are wrong – a visit to the High Force waterfall will do that – the evolutionists hide behind a façade that is not so easily penetrated, especially by children at school.

The method used in all scientific advances is to proceed outwards from areas of certain knowledge. Where frontiers are extended gradually by careful investigation the method works extremely well. Sometimes, however, there are sudden major advances which form the great stories of science: Newton's sudden advance in dynamics, leading to the development of celestial mechanics; the theory of light and of radiation in general in the nineteenth century; and quantum mechanics in the present century. The accolades given to those taking part in such advances are great, and they become household names. Rather naturally, it is the ambition of most scientists to become a leading figure in such a major advance. Some succeed by ability, others by luck, and still others, unhappily, by design and deception. The trick is to pretend that a major advance has been made, when in fact there has been none. To achieve such a deception, a cabal of scientists, rather than a lone individual is usually needed. Speaking with one voice, a cabal is often able to shout down lone individuals working in other directions and eventually, by gaining control over what material is published in scientific journals and what is not, a cabal can in the end wipe out all opposition.

Such situations cannot arise entirely by design. There must first be what in sport is often called the 'run of the ball'. Facts must at first sight appear to favour the line taken by the cabal. Design comes in when contradictory facts later appear and are deliberately suppressed through the control which the cabal has obtained over the scientific journals. When, furthermore, the cabal's views proceed to invade the educational system, becoming taught to large numbers of students, who, faced by the constant burden of difficult examinations, are not in a position to defend themselves, dogma becomes established. Society becomes saddled with a false area of supposed certain knowledge, which besides the damage it causes directly impedes the development of all nearby surrounding areas of science.

This same process happening simultaneously in many directions is what, more than any other factors, produces the decline, decay and ultimate collapse of human societies.

CHAPTER TWO

The Copernican Revolution begins

The concept of relative motion does not come easily to a young child. Most of us have childhood memories of sitting in a stationary train and seeing a train whiz past on the neighbouring track. When it had passed by, we could scarcely believe our eyes that our own train had not moved. This is a striking example from our day-to-day experience that could drive home the concept of relative motion, but it requires a degree of maturity to grasp. A child of three would be baffled, but for a child of ten it might well be an education.

The idea of the Earth spinning rapidly about an axis is even harder for a young child to accept. In everyday experience, the Earth does indeed seem immovable, a veritable terra firma, providing, perhaps, a strong sense of security. A child taking its first tentative steps learns quickly that the hard ground is always there under its feet to break every fall! It is little wonder, then, that human beings resisted the idea of a moving Earth for many centuries. The belief in a fixed Earth, an Earth impervious to all external influences, was written firmly into Christian dogma by the eighth century AD. The sky was regarded merely as an embellishment, consisting of a system of transparent crystal spheres on which the stars and planets were set like jewels. These beliefs were strongly held and vigorously defended;

disbelievers who dared question them were in danger of losing their lives. The result was that many plain facts of the world were often suppressed. It is quite remarkable that the supernova of AD 1054 that produced the Crab Nebula was not recorded in Western Europe, while it is described in Chinese records as attaining a brightness superior to Venus. Nor were naked-eye sunspots ever recorded in Europe, for the reason that it would have cast doubt on the perfection of heavenly bodies.

The turning point in this story of repression came in the autumn of 1496 when Domenico Maria da Novara, Professor of Astronomy at the University of Bologna, took on a twenty-two-year-old Polish student named Nicolas Copernicus (Koppernigk in its unlatinized form). As Novara addressed his freshmen on the received wisdom of the day one might well have seen Copernicus grimace in disbelief. 'It is widely thought,' Novara might have said, 'that the Earth is a sphere standing motionless at the centre of the Universe. Around the Earth moves the Moon, the Sun and the five planets. Beyond, but still quite near, turn the stars on a transparent crystal sphere . . . .' Novara may then have proceeded to explain why the motion of planets presented a complication in this simple scheme of things. Each planet wandered against the background of the stars, tracing a continuous pattern of loops. But notwithstanding this problem, the Earth-centred model was made to fit the data in the manner first discussed by Ptolemy in the second century AD. Following in the tradition of Aristotle (384–322 BC), he argued that the heavenly bodies must be perfect in every respect, and must move along the most perfect of geometrical shapes, the circle. The looped paths of the planets required a combination of small circles moving around a set of larger circles, which in turn move around the centre of the Universe, which is the Earth. These are the so-called epicycles and deferents of the Ptolemaic system. Ptolemy and his followers required a large number of different circles to account for the motions of the Moon, the Sun and the five known planets, circles often without any known body at their centres.

Copernicus began to despair at the ever-increasing complexity of the system as a whole. After acquainting himself with the ideas of another Greek astronomer, Aristarchus of Samos, who lived in the third century BC, he began to veer away from Ptolemy and seek an

17

alternative route. He contemplated the possibility that the Earth rotated around its own axis as well as about the Sun. But since he had no comprehension of gravity he continued to be baffled by the great speeds at the surface that would result from the rotation of the Earth. 'Surely, if the Earth is spinning so fast,' ran the popular argument, 'we should all be flung off its surface!'

Ignoring this difficulty, Copernicus set out to account for planetary motions by arguing that the other planets, besides the Earth, also circled around the Sun – Mars taking nearly two years and Jupiter almost 12 years to complete a full circuit. He worked assiduously on these ideas over the many years during which he served as private physician to his Uncle Lucas, the Bishop of Ermland, at Heilsberg Castle. Yet the finer details of planetary motions continued to elude him. The simple picture of motion around the Sun in circles failed to fit all the available data, and Copernicus reluctantly considered the idea of smaller circles moving upon larger ones, which made him wonder whether his own picture was really any simpler than Ptolemy's after all, so that his own account in 1512 was confined to a short synopsis, circulated only in manuscript form.

Partly because of his growing diffidence, but more particularly because the Roman Church was looking with increasing disfavour on the heliocentrism theory, Copernicus became increasingly reluctant to publish his theory in full. However, in his last years Copernicus was visited over an extended period by a young German, Georg Joachim Rheticus, who contrived to make a copy of Copernicus's ultimate manuscript. Carrying this copy back to Wittenberg, Rheticus arranged for it to be printed, apparently without the consent of its author and with a self-denigratory preface written by one Osiander. A copy of the book reached Poland only shortly before Copernicus's death in 1543, the preface causing much anger among his friends. Even so, the weight added to the ideas by the publication ultimately had its effect, although it took many years for the effect to show. It was to be fifty years from Copernicus to Kepler and almost another century to Newton, with Galileo's affray with the Church falling between Kepler and Newton, as we shall now describe. Copernicus was not to know that his work would initiate what would prove to be perhaps the most important revolution in the entire history of science. As we shall see later, distant rumblings of the same revolution are to be heard even in the present day.

The Sun-centred world-view was exceedingly slow to gain ground. Tycho Brahe (1546–1601) and Johannes Kepler (1571–1630) were the next actors in the great drama that was to follow. Kepler, a teacher of humble means in the town of Graz in Austria, published a refutation of Copernicus's theory of circles on circles in 1596. In its place he revived the idea of planets moving in simple circles around the Sun, attributing all the difficulties that Copernicus had experienced with this simpler model to erroneous or inaccurate observations. He thus took upon himself the difficult task of securing the best possible data on planetary motions to prove his point.

Kepler had heard of a Danish nobleman, Tycho Brahe, who was rumoured to possess the most modern and best-equipped observatory on his private island of Hven off the coast of Denmark. Brahe had amassed a wealth of accurate data on the positions of the planets over several years, and Kepler yearned to get hold of this precious data so that he could check his theory. Unfortunately, the distance from Graz to Hven was too great and the journey too expensive for the humble teacher to afford. Just as Kepler was despairing that he might never be able to check his theory, news came that Brahe had quarrelled with the Danish king and left Denmark. After two years of wandering across Europe, Brahe finally settled at Prague in 1599 and became official astronomer to the Emperor Rudolph II of Bohemia.

Fortunately Prague was near enough for Kepler to visit, and on 1 January 1600 he set off from his home town on a historic journey that was to change the course of science. The meeting between Kepler and Brahe which took place on 4 February 1600 was a disappointment for Kepler, however. Kepler had hoped for immediate results, but he found that Brahe was extremely possessive of his data, and gave only the vaguest inkling of what records he had. He succeeded in keeping Kepler at bay for the best part of a year; on one occasion Kepler left Prague in utter frustration. Subsequently, Kepler was appointed as Brahe's senior assistant at the observatory, but even then Brahe was not forthcoming about the full range of observations he possessed.

On 13 October 1601 Brahe died quite suddenly, and Kepler was appointed his successor. Kepler now had immediate and unimpeded access to all the data. He was hopeful that the matter could be resolved in a matter of weeks, but the task took a good deal longer. It was only some four years after Brahe's death that Kepler finally discovered that planetary orbits were ellipses rather than circles. An elegantly simple heliocentric model of the Solar System fell neatly into place, although the precise reason for elliptical orbits and the force that held the planets in such orbits remained a mystery.

Next on the scene was Galileo Galilei (1564–1642), Professor of Mathematics at the University of Padua. Galileo was informed by a former student, Jacques Badovere, of the invention of the telescope, an instrument which could make distant objects look near. He was informed that this instrument, said to have been discovered by a Dutch maker of eyeglasses named Hans Lippershey, consisted of two lenses, one convex and one concave, mounted at the ends of a long, hollow metal tube. Within months of the news, Galileo had successfully constructed the first prototype of a refracting astronomical telescope. On 8 August 1609, members of the Venetian Senate were invited to the tower of St Mark's Cathedral to gaze at ships through the new instrument. The senators were astounded to see incoming ships at sea several hours before they became visible to the naked eye. So impressed were the senators that they immediately doubled Galileo's salary as Professor of Mathematics.

Galileo spent many months improving his instrument in order to achieve higher magnifications. When he eventually turned the new telescope to the skies, the received wisdom of the day was instantly challenged in ways that could not have been imagined. To begin with, the telescope revealed many more stars than could be seen with the naked eye and a great deal of hitherto unsuspected facts emerged. On 7 January 1610 Galileo began a series of historic observations that ultimately revealed a system of satellites revolving around the planet Jupiter. Jupiter and its attendant satellites formed a miniature Solar System, a world within a world. Amongst a host of other findings, craters were discovered on the Moon; Venus and Mercury were found to have phases like the Moon; sunspots were discovered and recorded. Heavenly bodies were not constant, perfect, unchanging. Even the Sun was forced to reveal its blemishes, and the movement of these spots in one direction only indicated clearly that the Sun was spinning about an axis.

A thousand years of Church dogma came under threat with repercussions that were naturally to follow. The invention of the telescope opened up a new vision of the world. Galileo published a summary of his decisive new results in 1610 under the title *Siderus nuncius* ('The Starry Messenger'), and the new ideas soon became widely known. In the same year Galileo left Padua to become 'first philosopher and mathematician' to the Grand Duke of Tuscany.

The Church of Rome still held steadfastly to its traditional view that the Earth was stationary and the indisputable centre of the Universe. At first Galileo was cautious not to offend the Church, and avoided reference to this particularly sensitive point, but this restraint was not to last for long. As the evidence accumulated Galileo felt impelled to take on the Church, and in 1613 he argued that from the movement of spots across the face of the Sun it could be inferred that Copernicus was right and Ptolemy was wrong.

The Church was slow to react to this blow, and three years of soul-searching preceded the publication on 5 March 1616 of a decree banning Copernicus's book. Galileo also received a personal warning neither to 'hold nor defend' the Copernican doctrine. In 1624 he sought special permission from the Pope to write about 'the systems of the world', both Ptolemaic and Copernican, and permission was granted on condition that certain stipulations were observed.

Galileo's great work appeared in 1632, and the torrent of emotion that was unleashed could not be stemmed. The Pope heard from his advisors that, despite the noncommittal stance adopted by the author, the argument itself was presented in so compelling a manner in favour of the Copernican world-view that the authority of the Church was under the most serious threat. It was said that Galileo's new book would be potentially more damaging to the Church than the protestations of Luther and Calvin put together. In the crisis that followed, Galileo was ordered to Rome in 1633 to stand trial for heresy. At the trial he was convicted and sentenced to imprisonment for the crime of holding and teaching the Copernican doctrine. Eventually the Church showed a measure of leniency: upon reciting a statement

to the effect that he 'abjured, cursed and detested' his former indis-
cretions, Galileo had his sentence commuted to one of house arrest
at his own private estate at Arcetri near Florence, where he remained
until his death in 1642.

But no imprisonment or house arrest could stall the momentum
of the Copernican revolution. In the year of Galileo's death the next
crucial actor in this drama was born – the Englishman Isaac Newton
(1642–1727). After graduating from Cambridge in the summer of
1665, Newton found that the university was closed owing to the
outbreak of plague. He was forced to stay at home for nearly two
years, and it is probably during this period of seclusion that he first
began to address his mind to the problem of world systems. In
particular, he would have begun to ponder the question that was
unresolved in the Copernican theory: 'why it is that the planets go
round the Sun'?

Although Newton's formal astronomical education in Cambridge
was almost certainly confined to the Earth-centred Aristotelean
world-view, it is clear from his notebooks (which he began in the
year 1664) that he was well aware of the momentum of the scientific
revolution that was afoot. He was also aware of, and deeply influenced
by, the works of the French natural philosopher René Descartes,
who in contrast to Aristotle advocated a quantitative rather than a
qualitative view of the world.

Newton spent the plague years essentially arming himself with the
mathematical equipment he would use to discover the universal law
of gravitation and its consequences for planetary motion. By the time
he returned to Cambridge in 1667, as a Fellow of Trinity College,
he had already laid the foundations of the calculus and had also
derived the inverse square law of planetary attraction and the dynamics of circular motion. After many extensive diversions into optics
and the nature of light, he finally returned to a definitive discussion
of the theory of planetary orbits and Universal gravitation in the
years 1679–80, culminating in the publication of *The Mathematical
Principles of Natural Philosophy*, best known by the shortened form
of its original Latin title as the *Principia*.

Urged on by the astronomer Edmund Halley, Newton was finally
able to show that the new theory could account exactly for all the

known movements of objects in the Solar System, including comets. Using the Newtonian theory, Halley correctly predicted that a comet seen in the year 1682 would reappear in 1758. The comet was later named Comet Halley in his honour; we shall return to it in a later chapter. This successful prediction dealt a deathblow to the already enfeebled Ptolemaic model of the Solar System.

The success of the Copernican revolution was reluctantly conceded, at least as far as the Solar System was concerned. But what of the situation beyond? The next important step followed further refinements of observational techniques, in particular the invention of the reflecting telescope, also by Newton. Through the untiring efforts of William Herschel (1738–1822), it was discovered that the Milky Way was interspersed with thousands of nebulae, both bright and dark. The Sun, the centre of our planetary system, was soon relegated to the position of a single insignificant star among the billions of stars that populated the Milky Way. In the latter half of the nineteenth century and in the early years of the twentieth, an attempt was made to revive the pre-Copernican view of the Universe, but in a twice-displaced way. Although the Earth was not the centre of the Solar System, and although the Solar System was not the centre of the Milky Way, the Milky Way was to be the centre of the Universe, yet another error which many nevertheless argued passionately for, including distinguished astronomers. Yet again, the pre-Copernican outlook proved to be in error, as we suspect it always will be in whatever form it manifests itself, especially in the biological matters which form the main substance of this book.

CHAPTER THREE

From urine to organic soup

If life had not arisen on Earth, carbon would exist here as carbon dioxide, CO_2, and nitrogen as N_2, both of which are classified as inorganic substances. These key elements would never have combined as hydrides, as with carbon in methane, CH_4, and nitrogen in ammonia, NH_3. Bear this in mind as this chapter unfolds.

There are said to be about a million professional chemists in the world, and probably as many again who are students of the subject. We suspect there are few among this multitude who have any doubt that they know the difference between organic and inorganic chemistry. That surely 'everybody' knows the difference would be the likely response to a request for a definition. After all, students are given examination papers headed 'inorganic chemistry' and 'organic chemistry', so on the face of it the difference would seem to be well understood. But after making a search for definitions in standard textbooks and finding nothing precise, we are compelled to wonder exactly where in the educational system students are supposed to acquire this knowledge.

This is just the kind of information one expects to find in the *Encyclopaedia Britannica*, since articles there have been written by the world's great authorities. The writer of the *Encyclopaedia*'s article on general chemistry must have felt on awkward ground, for a somewhat transparent bluff is attempted. Organic chemistry is said to be the study of the molecular compounds of carbon, inorganic chemistry being by implication the study of compounds of elements other than carbon. Now, a counterexample is a device used in mathematics for disposing of dubious statements: it is an explicit case in which what is being asserted is untrue. The common gas carbon dioxide is always regarded as inorganic, and no student would complain if the properties of carbon dioxide appeared in an examination paper headed 'inorganic chemistry'. But carbon dioxide is obviously a compound of carbon. So the unemotive attempt of the *Encyclopaedia* to distinguish organic from inorganic fails. What goes on, then, one might wonder?

What goes on has historical connections with creationism. Organic material was regarded until the nineteenth century as stuff produced solely by living organisms. Inorganic material, on the other hand, was the stuff of the non-living world. Because the two were regarded as distinct, it was argued that life cannot be produced from non-life, and so life must have been created as such deliberately by a creator. This doctrine of 'vitalism' is said in writings on the history of chemistry to have been destroyed by Friedrich Wöhler in 1828. Wöhler synthesized urea, a principal component of urine, from ammonium cyanate. At the time, urea was regarded as organic because of its presence in the excretion products of animals, while everybody accepted that ammonium cyanate was inorganic. So here was a supposed counterexample, proving, it was said, that organic material can indeed be made from inorganic material. Exit vitalism, to the delight of its many opponents.

To begin with, the case against vitalism seemed reasonably argued, but with the discovery of bacteria (following Louis Pasteur's work on silkworm disease and the fermentation of alcoholic liquids), the situation darkened perceptibly. The ammonium radical in the ammonium cyanate used by Wöhler in his preparation of urea came from some naturally occurring deposit of an ammonium salt. But where had such a deposit come from? And in particular, where had the nitrogen in the ammonium radical come from?

With the application of chemistry to agriculture becoming of greater and greater relevance to society, it eventually emerged that nitrogen in the atmosphere is the source of nitrogen in the soil, and that it is the growth of certain kinds of plant (e.g. peas and beans) that causes this change of venue for the nitrogen. Nitrogen passes from air to ground through the action of plants, not through the action of inorganic processes (except possibly in very small quantities: for example, small quantities of nitrogen oxides might be produced in lightning flashes and become subsequently washed out of the air into the soil). When plants responsible for this so-called fixing of nitrogen die, their remains are acted on by bacteria, and the ammonium radical is produced as a by-product. Hence deposits of ammonium salts in the soil are overwhelmingly the result of the action of denitrifying bacteria, and the ammonium cyanate used by Wöhler was therefore almost surely of biological origin. The supposed preparation of an organic material from an inorganic one was therefore an illusion, for the supposed inorganic material was not truly inorganic: it had a biological and therefore an organic source. Wöhler had used a material with an organic origin to prepare another organic material, which was not what the anti-vitalistic argument had claimed. Seen in broader perspective, life had been used to make the ammonium cyanate, and there was nothing anti-vitalistic in that because the intervention of biological organisms was just what the vitalists had always claimed to be necessary.

When these further facts eventually came to light, chemists and biologists did not review the matter as they should have done. They did not apologize to the vitalists for a mistake which began inadvertently, but which by the end of the nineteenth century had become quite distinctly deliberate. The deliberate mistake continues to this day. Every chemistry student is still given the wrong interpretation of Wöhler's experiment. This is an example of the illusions and dogmas in the education system discussed in Chapter 1.

From 1908, when Fritz Haber first proposed an industrial process for the fixing of atmospheric nitrogen, consciences could be assuaged a little. The idea was to pass a mixture of hydrogen and nitrogen over a suitable catalyst. This is done nowadays at high temperature and pressure over an iron catalyst, a process much used in the production of artificial fertilizer. It was this process which permitted Germany to fight the First World War, since without it there would not have been an adequate supply of nitrogenous explosives. It is usual to think of the Haber–Bosch process, as it is called nowadays, as inorganic. If this were true, one could take the ammonia thus produced and use it to produce ammonium cyanate inorganically, and so back to Wöhler's synthesis of urea. But a little thought soon shows that industrial hydrogen is always obtained from a biological material, so the inorganic nature of the Haber–Bosch process is yet another illusion. Coal was used to obtain the hydrogen originally, but nowadays hydrocarbons are used – both coal and hydrocarbons being overtly of biological origin. A more subtle way to obtain hydrogen would be through the electrolysis of water, that is to say, the breaking-up of water molecules by means of electric currents. But, discounting electrolysis caused by lightning flashes, the electricity necessary for electrolysis is man-made and therefore biological also. And naturally occurring lightning flashes cause almost no electrolysis at all.

By following trains of thought such as these, it can be shown that the old vitalistic doctrine is very nearly true. No way has yet been found for converting *truly* inorganic materials to organic ones in anything other than trace quantities without the intervention of living organisms. When this does happen, enormous amounts of organic material can be produced, at great speed in favourable conditions. The prospects for converting inorganic materials to organic appear to be worse in space than on the Earth, because inorganic catalysts which on Earth have to be prepared with the greatest care would be quickly poisoned under astronomical conditions by corrosive gases, by sulphur compounds in particular. In space, pressures are low, while in the atmospheres of planets like Jupiter and Saturn temperatures are low, causing inorganic reactions to be slowed to a crawl.

These remarks provide the background to the rest of this chapter, which examines the all-important question of how, according to present scientific lore, life is supposed to have begun. Let us first see how the case is usually presented, before we come to the holes in the argument. In 1952–3 Stanley Miller and Harold Urey performed an experiment which seemed at the time to support the idea that life could have originated gradually from inorganic chemical substances. The experiment was based on a recreation of the physical conditions that were supposed to have prevailed on the newly formed Earth about 4 billion years ago. It was thought that an atmosphere existed that would be poisonous to most modern life-forms: methane, ammonia, carbon monoxide and dioxide, nitrogen and possibly hydrogen cyanide, together with an ample supply of water. Conditions were taken to be highly disturbed, with frequent huge electrical storms and much volcanic activity.

In the experiment, high-voltage sparks were passed through a mixture of gases representing the supposed early terrestrial atmosphere, often for many days at a time. The results were widely applauded as demonstrating almost beyond doubt the answer to the question of the origin of life. Many organic life-associated molecules were found in the resultant 'soup', among which were two basic biochemical building blocks: amino acids – the constituents of proteins – and nitrogenous bases, constituents of DNA.

This first experiment was followed by others, and by now a large number of different organic molecules have been obtained. In the Earth's early oceans and lakes these molecules would have accumulated, it is argued, because there were no living organisms to consume them. The oceans would have been brimming with complex organic molecules, with about a third of the concentration found in chicken broth, whence the term 'organic soup'.

All this is dreadfully wrong, however. The methane used by Urey and Miller was almost surely obtained from natural gas, and so was of biological origin. The ammonia was also of suspect origin, just as it was in Wöhler's experiment. So what was actually done was to start with biomaterials and from them produce other biomaterials, a far less impressive outcome than it seemed at the time. If Urey and Miller, and their successors, had used only materials that were genuinely inorganic in the *terrestrial* context and had obtained similar results, the achievement would have been more impressive. The correct materials to use would have been water, nitrogen, and carbon monoxide and dioxide, for the reason that these substances might have occurred quite naturally on the early Earth before the onset of biological processes.

We have serious doubts, moreover, even about the claim to have produced high concentrations of life-associated molecules, a claim made in our view without adequate documentation by later investigators. What we think happened was the following. Suppose one thinks of a long experiment divided into many episodes. In each episode a small amount of life-associated material is produced, extracted and set aside, so being protected from the destructive effect of the high-voltage sparks occurring in subsequent episodes. Such a procedure, given enough episodes, might well produce the claimed high concentration, but under conditions without relevance to a natural state of affairs, where life-associated molecules would break up as fast as they were produced. It is precisely their inherent lack of stability, compared with water, nitrogen and carbon monoxide, which gives such molecules their life-associated properties. Deliberately setting aside the organic molecules, protecting them from disruption, would be a deception. It would be equivalent to what in physics is called introducing Maxwell's demon. Maxwell's demon is like Aladdin's genie. Given Maxwell's demon, almost anything becomes possible – like making one half of an ice-cold room grow hot without supplying heat or energy from outside the room.

Deceptions in science come in two forms: overt and inadvertent; another name for overt deception is of course cheating. Deceptions often begin as inadvertent and then later become overt. It was inadvertent that Urey and Miller did not realize the essence of life to be its structure, not its building blocks. It is the precision arrangements of different amino acids in long chains that is the big issue. To take just one example, the protein histone-4 has essentially the same chain of 102 amino acids in all life-forms. If you had random shots at assembling this particular chain from a supply of individual amino acids to suit yourself – one shot for every atom in every star in every galaxy visible in the largest telescopes, your chance of successfully finding histone-4 would be like backing a horse at odds of 5×10^{132} (that is, 5 followed by 132 zeros) to 1 against, and histone-4 is just one of very many critical proteins.

In 1952–3 the science of microbiology was still in its infancy, and so Urey and Miller knew nothing of the real heart of the problem of the origin of life when they carried out their first experiment. Consequently it seemed exciting to find some of the building blocks of life emerging from that experiment. Today, almost half a century on, so much is known about the structures of complex biomolecules like histone-4, and the essence of life can be seen to lie in the many remarkable properties which arise from the arrangements of the basic building blocks, which themselves can be quite simple.

This is distinctively the case for sugars and their derivatives. Carbon monoxide and hydrogen are the two commonest molecules in the Universe. Combine one of each and you have a molecule of form-aldehyde, possessing only a very slight measure of stability against splitting apart into carbon monoxide and hydrogen, a property with astonishing consequences. It is just because the normal human stance is upright, in a position with little stability, that an expert human skier can ski a downhill race on an uneven snow-covered mountain side. The horse stands in a very stable position, but fit four skis to the hooves of a horse and set it off on the same downhill run ... it would be hopeless!

The same is true for molecules. Because molecules near the margin of stability can go in many directions, remarkable things can happen. Liquid formaldehyde is somewhat unpleasant stuff in which biological specimens are often preserved. But take a number of formaldehyde molecules, usually five or six, join them together with a few inter-changes of atoms, and you have a sugar, the sweet stuff of chocolate. Still more remarkable, carrying out the joining and interchange processes in various ways will produce all the sugars, including the particular case of ribose. A derivative of ribose – deoxyribose – is what the D stands for in DNA. So here is another building block of life, a block that when analysed into smaller components can be seen to be a product of the commonest molecules in the Universe.

Joining similar sugar molecules with linking oxygen atoms produces the class of substances known as carbohydrates, with differ-ent sugar molecules giving different carbohydrates. One gives starch, the basic foodstuff of much of animal life. Another gives cellulose, which plays a critical role in giving mechanical strength to plants, permitting trees to grow to heights of a hundred metres and more, and providing the wood without which most man-made buildings would look very bare. Joining sugars via nitrogen-atom links yields yet another class of substances, including the hard material of a lobster shell and the beaks of birds.

Only six of the chemical elements play major parts in the basic structures of living organisms: hydrogen, carbon, nitrogen, oxygen, phosphorus and sulphur. Pairs of sulphur atoms join in a strong disulphide bond, and it is these bonds, often situated at widely separated places in the chain of amino acids forming a protein, that give a comparative rigidity to the characteristic shape into which a protein curls, a characteristic shape that is crucial to its biochemical properties. Disulphide bonds in a protein have to be just right if the protein is to behave in an interesting way, serving as a catalyst (far more effectively than man-made catalysts) in a biochemical process which may be crucial to life. There are thousands of examples of proteins crucial to life, each one depending on shapes which have to be just right.

Phosphorus plays a role in DNA somewhat similar to that of sulphur in proteins. Together with oxygen, phosphorus links the deoxyribose molecules into a structure whose shape is crucial, the famous double helix. But it is not just a question of obtaining any old double helix: the two component helices have to be correctly positioned with respect to each other so as to permit only one set of ties and their matching counterparts to join them. If linking ties could occur higgledy-piggledy, DNA could not carry information, and there would be no genetic code – just as there would be no information in writing if the letters of the alphabet were sprayed around higgledy-piggledy. Phosphorus plays a critical role in ensuring that this does not happen.

In addition to the six main chemical elements of life, there are 16 others which are present in living systems in smaller quantities, minor actors who nevertheless are important to the play during the moments they are on stage. Magnesium atoms, each held individually between six nitrogen atoms in the green substance chlorophyll, builds sugar molecules by photosynthesis. This is a device for going against the thermodynamic tendency of a chemical system to seek its lowest energy level, which necessarily applies to systems wholly at terrestrial temperature, say 25°C. The trick is to use light from the Sun, a source with a temperature of about 5500°C, thereby standing ordinary thermodynamics for 25°C on its head. By synthesizing sugars a potential source of energy is created, a source that is subsequently used in an inverse sense (sugars breaking down into their constituents), either by plants themselves or by animals that eat the plants. A similar arrangement with individual iron atoms, each held between four nitrogen atoms, provides the active centre of haemoglobin. The critical property again has reversibility, the reversibility of both storing and yielding a supply of oxygen, which again is used by animals in the release of energy. The element calcium plays a very different part, however. It is used to give strength to bones and, as calcium carbonate, to form the shells of many sea creatures. And so on for the other, often highly specialized activities of the remaining 13 elements.

Seen in retrospect, to have produced some of the building blocks of life in experiments of the Urey–Miller type was of no relevance to the origin of life, especially as some of the materials used in the experiments were already biological in origin, since no one doubts that life can give rise to life. The building blocks of life are commonplace. It is the structures to which they can give rise that are remarkable, and where the problem of the origin of life really lies. Not to have realized this in 1952–3 was understandable, but not to realize it today is inexcusable. Not to realize it today amounts to overt deception, at least on the part of research scientists who have ample time and opportunity to study the matter in depth. Students, on the other hand, can be excused, yet likely enough it will be from students that a general realization of the deceit will first come.

The deceit has strong motivation. It is to avoid the question of whether the situation, as facts have uncovered it to be, can sensibly be regarded as accidental. Is it reasonable to suppose that the commonest elements should by chance alone have such a range of properties as have been determined from biochemical studies, as for instance in the properties of enzymes? Or is there a teleological component, a purposive component, even in the properties of the chemical elements, let alone in the origin and development of life? If so, we are instantly thrown into very deep waters indeed. The creationist exclaims forcibly, to the point of shouting, that there is indeed a purposive component, while the *soi-disant* respectable scientist shows, not by shouting but by tricks, that of course it is not so. A typical trick is the so-called anthropic principle – that if the situation is not exactly the way we find it we would not be here to discuss it. Therefore, remarkable as the accidents may look at first sight, our presence is a guarantee that they occurred. But our presence could just as well be a guarantee that life is purposive, planned. The situation is decidedly unproven, with the anthropic principle no more than a tautology.

Both the creationist and the *soi-disant* respectable scientist, by attempting to decide the matter without reference to the facts, or to decide it by distorting the facts, are in a sense guilty of blasphemy. Neither is likely in our view to contribute much to progress.

CHAPTER FOUR

Organic material everywhere

Organic material exists everywhere throughout our Milky Way system, our galaxy. Indeed, most of the non-stellar material in our galaxy consists either of hydrogen and helium gas or of small, solid organic grains with sizes very similar to the typical sizes of bacteria. Under very dry conditions, at low pressure, the water which occupies about 70 per cent of the interior volumes of bacteria under normal terrestrial conditions would evaporate away, leaving particles that were mostly hollow. And we know from highly accurate astronomical measurements that the organic grains which are widespread throughout the vast spaces between the stars of our galaxy are indeed hollow. Their combined mass is vast. Adding together the individual small masses of the huge number of interstellar grains yields a total that is more than 10^{12} times the mass of the Earth.

In view of the impossibility of producing cosmically, by non-biological means, organic material from inorganics like water, carbon monoxide and dioxide, and nitrogen gas, it is clear that the immense amount of interstellar organics must be biological in origin. Some scientists have tried to maintain otherwise, but this is to carry dogma to extreme lengths. If no more than trace quantities of organics can be produced from inorganics even under carefully adjusted laboratory conditions, especially using carefully prepared catalysts, large quantities will not be produced in uncontrolled conditions where prospective catalysts would be immediately poisoned, for instance by the corrosive sulphur, a common element that exists everywhere.

Another major objection to the production of organics from inorganics by nonbiological means is that production processes used in our chemical industry are all of what one might call a linear kind. A chemical company wishing to double its output must double its productive capacity by building more plant capacity, which is why the chemical industry as it expands has to generate more and more capital. The capacity needed to produce a mass of chemicals equal to that of the Earth would be unimaginably large, even if many years were allowed for its operation. Biological systems, on the other hand, have a crucially different mode of expansion. Instead of being linear, they are exponential in character – one makes two, two makes four, four makes eight, and so on. Biological expansion is explosive, becoming more and more extreme as it feeds on itself.

Let us start with a single bacterium, and suppose that it and its progeny are supplied with suitable nutrients. A typical time for replication under favourable conditions would be two or three hours. In a day, the initial bacterium would have expanded by one makes two, two makes four . . ., each step requiring two or three hours, into a colony of about 1000 bacteria, still much too small to be seen by the unaided eye. In two days the 1000 bacteria would become 1,000,000, a colony just visible to the eye, about a tenth of the diameter of a pinhead. In four days the original bacterium would have become 1,000,000,000,000 bacteria, together weighing about a gram. In five days the colony would be approaching a kilogram in weight. So it would proceed, with three zeros added to the numbers for every day that passed: a tonne after six days, 1000 tonnes after a week, the mass of Mount Everest after eleven days, that of the Earth after thirteen days, our galaxy after nineteen days, and the whole of the visible Universe in twenty-two days – roughly a three-week job, starting with the single bacterium. With such an immense potential for expansion available, only an obscurantist would seek to explain the immense quantity of organic material in our galaxy by any means other than biological. No problem exists about the mode of production of the organic matter, only about its location. We have to find the places where the environmental conditions favour explosive bacterial expansion.

The places cannot be interstellar space, judging from the requirements for bacterial replication found here on the Earth. Either the presence of liquid water or an atmosphere with relative humidity above 60 per cent is usually found necessary for the replication of microorganisms (although diatoms have been reported to replicate in ice). The temperature range for replication appears to be typically from about minus 20°C to plus 80°C, although the presence of living bacteria at temperatures of up to 300°C in deep-sea 'black smoker' chimneys associated with volcanic vents shows that the upper limit of temperature probably exceeds 80°C by a considerable margin under high pressures.

A supply of suitable nutrients is of course also essential. Depending on the species of bacterium, nutrients can vary widely. It is the essential characteristic of a large class of so-called chemo-autotrophic bacteria that they replicate from inorganic substances alone. Indeed, one can say that wherever inorganic substances exist under natural conditions with the possibility of energy being obtained from them by a chemical reaction, then a bacterium exists to exploit the situation. This is provided the reaction occurs only very slowly under purely inorganic conditions. Otherwise the opportunity for bacteria would not exist, because the reaction would occur inorganically and the substances, the nutrients, would be gone. Chemo-autotrophic bacteria manage to exploit energy-producing reactions that are otherwise too slow to happen inorganically by nonbiological means. The trick is to speed up such reactions immensely by the use of extremely subtle catalysts, the proteins called enzymes. Granted that only a little energy is available, so little that inorganic reactions cannot unlock it, bacteria can live on almost anything, which they do through the amazing properties of proteins.

Bacteria are exceedingly hardy in every respect one can think of. They have remarkable tolerance to temperature, to pressure, to nutrients and to radiation damage. In the latter respect the following extract from a publication by the present writers and others summarizes the situation:

It is established that many species are capable of thriving in environments containing extremely high concentrations of unusually lethal radioisotopes such as americium, plutonium, strontium, etc. Diatoms thrive in highly radioactive ponds including the U-pond and the Z-trench at the Hanford facility, with the latter containing over 8 kg of various radioisotopes of plutonium. Not only do diatoms and bacteria live in this environment but they seem to have a remarkable affinity for plutonium.... The algae of these ponds, of which diatoms are by far the dominant form, concentrate Am three millionfold, and certain isotopes of plutonium are accumulated to 400 million times the concentration in the surrounding water. The plant life in these radioactive ponds contains more than 95% of the total plutonium burden. Diatoms and *Potamogeton* alone contain more than 99% of this plutonium. In such an environment, diatoms grow in great abundance while continuously subjected to high levels of X-rays, gamma rays, alpha and beta particles. (R. B. Hoover, F. Hoyle, N. C. Wickramasinghe, M. J. Hoover and S. Al-Mufti, *Earth, Moon and Planets*, 1986, **35,** 19)

The properties of bacteria are not at all of the kind that could possibly be explained by evolution in a terrestrial environment, because in many respects their properties have no relation to conditions encountered naturally on the Earth, for instance in their resistance to exceedingly low temperatures and pressures, and their resistance to immense doses of destructive radiation. There has never been a terrestrial environment in which such properties could have evolved, and so, according to the Darwinian mode of evolution they simply should not exist. But in fact they do.

Microorganisms recover from damage to their basic genetic material in a subtle way. The method of repair turns on there being two helices in DNA. Damage at a particular site on the DNA nearly always occurs to only one of the two helices and/or its attachments. A battery of enzymes is first called out to remove the damaged region. Then other enzymes take a look at the undamaged helix and its attachments, from which it is possible to work out what the site of the damaged helix (now removed) should properly be. With the proper form decided, enzymes first construct a correct new bit of helix together with the correct attachments to it. This is fitted into place, and the double helix is returned to its proper form. No such complex process could possibly arise, in our opinion, unless there had been an imperative necessity for it – such as certainly exists in space but not on the Earth, where biological systems are shielded by the atmosphere from the critical source of damage in space, namely X-rays of solar and cosmic origin. Biological systems on the Earth can be hit by a cosmic-ray particle, but such events for a target as small as a microorganism are exceedingly rare. No complex process of repair is required for rare events, since an assembly of bacteria with immense powers of replication could easily afford the wholly trivial losses that would arise from un-likely accidents. Humans, with their vastly larger target area for cosmic rays and other stray low-level sources of damage, manage quite well without having a repair mechanism to equal that of bacteria.

Let us now look at where bacteria can replicate. Interstellar space is evidently ruled out, both because of the extreme conditions that prevail there and for the reasons discussed above. We are thus led logically to look to conditions in the vicinities of stars. We can conceive of microorganisms, a fraction of them viable, being brought by astronomical processes to the vicinity of stars where, given suitable conditions, they replicate explosively. A fraction of the newly rep-licated organisms is returned to interstellar space in accordance with the cyclic process illustrated in Figure 4.1.

Planets are far more substantial objects than comets, so that at first one might think that planets would be more suitable places for biological replication than comets. But what one planet gains on one comet in size and mass is lost in their relative numbers. In the Solar System, there are, it is generally believed by astronomers, billions of times more comets than planets. Taken together, the collective mass of comets is comparable to that of a giant planet like Uranus or Neptune, a considerably greater mass than the Earth. Far from being ruled out on grounds of size, comets collectively provide places that in the most important respects appear superior to planets. A fraction of the comets in the Solar System, like Comet Halley, occasionally or periodically approach the Sun, which can produce evaporation of gas and dust at a rate of about a million tonnes per day. The dust, in the form of bacteria and other microorganisms, is partly expelled from the Solar System into interstellar space (so forming the lower arc of

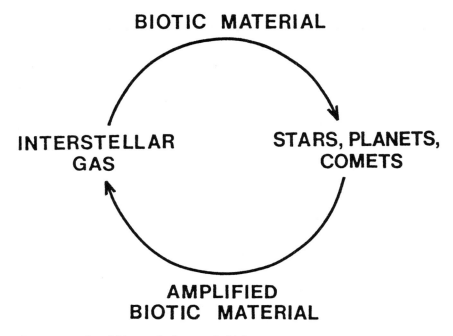

BIOTIC MATERIAL

INTERSTELLAR GAS

STARS, PLANETS, COMETS

AMPLIFIED BIOTIC MATERIAL

Figure 4.1 Amplifying cycle for cosmic biology.

Figure 4.1) and is partly available for seeding planets like the Earth with life.

Before resting content with this picture of the mode of origin of bacteria in space, we have to ask whether the lower arc of Figure 4.1 really could be strong enough to populate interstellar space with the immense amount of granular material that is found there. If the possession of planets and comets by the Sun is regarded as a typical property of all so-called dwarf stars like the Sun, the situation can be shown to be just right. Explicitly, the combined mass of comets in the Solar System (taken to be equal to that of Uranus or Neptune) is about 10^{29} grams, and there are about 10^{11} dwarf stars in our galaxy. The product of these numbers is 10^{40} grams, which is just the combined mass of all the interstellar grains.

According to the dogma prevailing up to the recent approach of Comet Halley, comets were supposed to be 'dirty snowballs', not residues of intense biological activity. Water would of course be present in considerable quantities, whether in a snowball or in a biological system. To decide between the two points of view it was necessary therefore to examine the components of a comet other than water. Evidence from the 1960s favoured the organic hypothesis, so in fact there was never any ground for the 'dirty snowball' dogma,

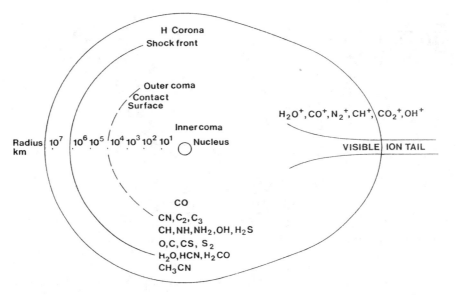

Figure 4.2 A pre-1986 (pre-Halley) depiction of the distribution of small molecules and ions in the coma of a typical comet (adapted from J. C. Brandt and R. D. Chapman, *Introduction to Comets*, Cambridge University Press, 1981). More recent data from direct sampling of Comet Halley shows an ensemble of molecules exceedingly rich in complex organic molecules.

if by 'dirt' one meant ordinary dirt. It was found long ago that present in the gases emitted by comets were all manner of molecules containing a small number of atoms, usually two or three of the same kind, that would be expected to appear when complex organic molecules break into fragments. The types of small molecule actually detected in comets *before* the 1986 return of Comet Halley are shown in Figure 4.2, and they are not at all what would be expected from the break-up of inorganic materials. Nothing like them could be expected from the disintegration of, for example, simple inorganic ices or bits of household dust. The recently discovered molecule with two sulphur atoms, S_2, is particularly interesting in relation to the disulphide linkages which play so important a role in protein structure.

The encounter with Comet Halley on its return to the inner regions of the Solar System established several critically important results:

1 The particles which emerged from the comet at a rate of about a million tonnes per day when it was in an active condition had compositions dominated by the elements hydrogen, carbon, nitrogen and oxygen. Since the particles did not evaporate away at temperatures as high as 50°C, they would not be inorganic compounds of these elements, like water and ammonia, and so they were almost surely of an organic nature.

2 Many of the particles have sizes typical of bacteria.

3 The particles had low densities consistent with them being hollow, as bacteria would be after the water initially within them had evaporated away.

4 The particles had infrared properties for wavelengths between 3 and 4 micrometres that were closely similar to the properties of bacteria.

5 In respect of points 2, 3 and 4, the particles were also closely similar to the interstellar grains between the stars.

6 Organic molecules of much greater complexity than those in Figure 4.2 were found in the break-up products from the dust of Comet Halley.

Points 1, 2 and 3 were established through experiments carried out in the vicinity of Comet Halley by the teams of scientists responsible for the two Soviet Vega spacecraft (encounters on 6 and 9 March 1986) and the European probe, Giotto (encounter 14 March 1986), details of which were first reported in the 15 May issue of the journal *Nature*. Points 4 and 5 were established by D. T. Wickramasinghe and D. A. Allen using the Anglo-Australian Telescope in New South Wales, Australia.

To understand the force of points 4 and 5, consider for a moment the graph shown in Figure 4.3a. Wavelength is plotted in micrometres across the top of the chart. The scale on the left gives the fraction (as a percentage) of radiation of the various wavelengths which penetrated a sample of the common bacterium *Escherichia coli*. The graph was obtained by Shirwan Al-Mufti, and it is shown here just as it came off the pen-recorder in the laboratory. (This is important, because much of the supposed data one gets in science nowadays is not proper data at all, it is data that has been imaginatively redrawn, supposedly to make its import clearer, but perhaps for other reasons as well.)

It happens by the greatest of good fortune that almost exactly the same experiment is performed in an astronomical laboratory. At the centre of our galaxy there is a source of infrared radiation which acts like the source in the laboratory experiment. On its journey from the galactic centre to the Earth, the infrared radiation passes through a succession of grains stretching all the way from the Earth to the galactic centre, thereby sampling the grains very broadly. When the radiation reaches the Earth it can be examined with the aid of a large telescope, and the fraction at various wavelengths that has managed to penetrate the interstellar grains can be measured, just as in the laboratory experiment.

Suppose now that the interstellar grains really are bacteria. If they are, they will have absorption properties similar to those of the specimen used to obtain Figure 4.3a. What in that case would one expect the astronomical observations to reveal? The answer to this question is provided by the curve in Figure 4.3b, in which is plotted, against wavelength, the flux of radiation (on an arbitrary scale) received at the Earth from a powerful source of infrared radiation (GC-IRS7) near the centre of our galaxy. (A detail which it is necessary to take account of in obtaining the curve of Figure 4.3b is that, whereas the laboratory equipment uses a source of radiation that is effectively 'flat' with respect to wavelength, the astronomical source is thermal. This is why there are small differences between the two curves.) The points plotted in Figure 4.3b are the results obtained

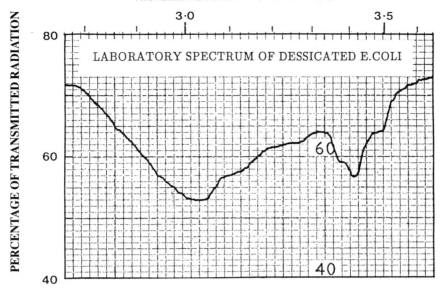

Figure 4.3a The transmittance spectrum of infrared radiation penetrating a potassium bromide disc containing 1.5 milligrams of the desiccated bacterium *E. coli*.

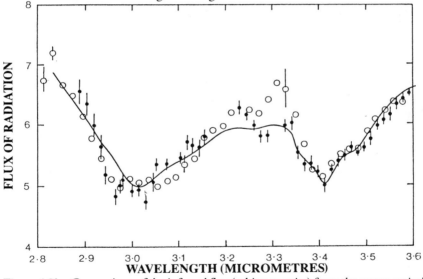

Figure 4.3b Comparison of the infrared flux (arbitrary units) from the astronomical source GC-IRS7 located near the galactic centre, with the curve predicted for dry *E. coli*. The open circles are the results of observations by Professor H. Okuda and his colleagues in Tokyo, and the filled points are the data of D. T. Wickramasinghe and D. A. Allen.

with the telescope, the bars through the points giving possible error ranges estimated by the observers. The agreement between the curve through the laboratory data in Figure 4.3*a* and the observations made by two quite independent teams of observers and recorded in Figure 4.3*b* is strengthened by the fact that the predictions were available in advance of the observations being made.

What can be said for certain from Figure 4.3*b* is that the interstellar grains must have absorption properties in this particular wavelength range that are closely similar to those in Figure 4.3*a*, similar to within about one small graticule division at every wavelength from 3 to 4 micrometres. Is there any other organic material of a nonbiological nature that satisfies this quite rigorous constraint? If not, then we can infer that the interstellar grains really are bacteria. We ourselves have examined many hundreds of spectra of potentially abundant organic compounds, and we have obtained scores of others in the laboratory. Yet we have found no other remotely suitable candidate when considered over the whole wavelength range. Some chemists have said differently, but without producing measured results with anything like the degree of precision necessary for their claims to be testable. The circumstance that vague statements on this matter have been permitted repeatedly at scientific meetings, no proof being offered either of fact or *bona fides*, shows how far many scientists are prepared to depart from proper standards when well-entrenched dogmas are threatened.

For some time there have been strong indications of the presence of highly complex biochemicals associated with interstellar grains. For nearly half a century astronomers have known that about twenty diffuse interstellar absorption features at well-defined wavelengths show up in the spectra of stars. Despite a great deal of effort on the part of many talented astronomers and physicists, the origin of these bands has remained a mystery: no inorganic material has been found with the required spectral fingerprints. Then in 1967, almost out of the blue, an American chemist, F. M. Johnson, showed by an elegant and well-thought-out experiment that a molecule closely related to chlorophyll would fit the bill extremely well. Chlorophyll, responsible for the green colouring of plant and algal cells, is of course a vital link in the whole chain of terrestrial life. Agreements in the positions of the characteristic wavelengths were so precise that one might have thought the proposed identification would have carried some measure of conviction. In fact, Johnson's pioneering contribution to this important problem has largely been ignored. Astronomers have continued to pretend among themselves that this solution does not exist.

More recent astronomical evidence, from both infrared and ultra-violet observations, have also shown that aromatic molecules

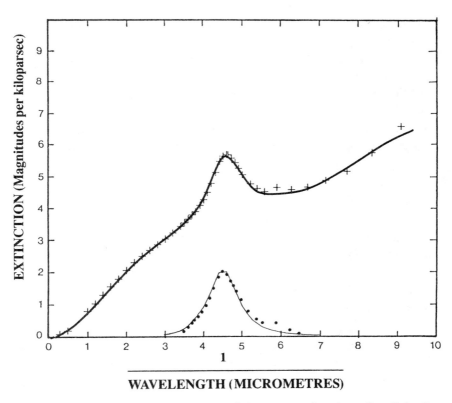

WAVELENGTH (MICROMETRES)

Figure 4.4 Crosses represent measures of the average dimming of starlight (in magnitudes per 1000 parsecs) by interstellar dust; the heavy solid curve is the calculated curve for a model involving hollow bacterial particles and aromatic molecules. Below it, the points represent the interstellar absorption around the 0.2175 micrometre wavelength region (corresponding to 4.6 on the reciprocal scale) and the thin curve is the prediction for biological aromatic molecules.

(molecules containing carbon rings, which are important in living material) must exist in great profusion in interstellar space. The fit of a bacterial model including such aromatic molecules to ultraviolet observations of the dimming of starlight is shown in Figure 4.4. The agreement is seen to be exceedingly close. Yet astronomers have stubbornly denied that this evidence could have any connection with life molecules outside the Earth, and have instead sought highly implausible, nonbiological alternatives.

In order to support the standard dogma, it has been claimed that esoteric substances with properties like those shown in Figure 4.3 can be obtained by exposing a mixture of materials such as methane, ammonia and water to fluxes of ultraviolet light and/or high-speed particles. Many of these experiments suffer from the defect, as did the Urey–Miller experiment, that the starting materials contain substances that must have been produced biologically from the mixture of inorganic materials that one would expect to find on an abiotic Earth. So, from a point of view of normal logic, claims to make these substances in an abiotic setting are already flawed. In some experiments that we are aware of, the chosen irradiation conditions are so extreme that they cannot conceivably be obtained under astronomical circumstances over an extensive scale. Furthermore, we have noticed that published spectra have all been of poor quality. Since only a milligram of material is needed to obtain the far higher quality of Figure 4.3, it is clear that the experiments in question did not succeed in producing so much as a milligram of an esoteric substance, which is then claimed to occupy the whole galaxy to an amount of 10^{43} milligrams.

Students of physics and chemistry learn early in their work that the same substance can produce either absorption or emission, according to circumstances. A cool gas intervening between the observer and a hot source of light like the Sun produces absorption, usually at more or less discrete wavelengths called 'lines'. The same substance, when itself heated, and without any background source of light, produces the same 'lines' but in emission, now appearing bright against a dark background. Solids have a similar ability to either absorb or emit radiation according to circumstances, except that solids emit and absorb over broad wavelength ranges instead of at discrete lines.

Thus the bacteria producing the absorption shown in Figure 4.3*a*, when viewed against a background of infrared radiation, would emit radiation in an inverted way if heated without a background source being present, an inversion that would rise to a maximum where, in Figure 4.3*a*, the absorption is a minimum, close to a wavelength of 3.4 micrometres.

The curve in Figure 4.5 shows the expected emission corresponding to the absorption in Figure 4.3*a* for bacteria heated to 47°C, which is a reasonable temperature for the particles emitted from Comet Halley on 31 March 1986, when the comet was at about the same distance from the Sun as the Earth is, about 150 million kilometres. The points in Figure 4.5 represent observations, made with the Anglo-Australian Telescope, of infrared radiation emitted by a cloud of small particles in the vicinity of the nucleus of the comet. The agreement between the bacterial model and the observations is again most striking. Indeed, we can say with certainty that particles ejected from Comet Halley have infrared properties over the wavelength range from 3 to 4 micrometres that are the same as those of bacteria to within an accuracy of about one small graticule division of Figure 4.3*a*, and in this respect we can say that particles ejected from Comet Halley were very like the interstellar grains.

Infrared radiation from particles around Comet Halley was also measured on 30 March and 1 April 1986. On both these days the emission was distinctly weaker than on 31 March, implying that the clouds of particles – estimated to have a total mass of about a million tonnes – observed on 31 March were ejected by the comet during the previous twelve hours or so, and that by 1 April the clouds had largely spread out, dissipating into surrounding space. Comets would therefore seem to be capable of spewing out bacteria at a rate of about a million tonnes per day, and that is a lot of bacteria.

It came as an even greater surprise when more recent explorations of Comet Halley revealed that this prodigious output of particles continued even when the comet had retreated beyond the orbit of Jupiter. A modest-sized dust halo was observed in February 1990, and an enormous elongated dust halo with a total mass of 100,000 tonnes developed in the period February–April 1991. To the aston-

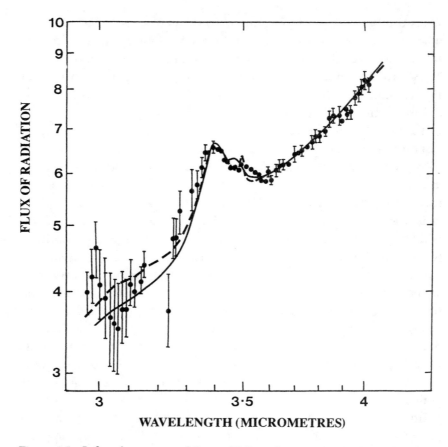

Figure 4.5 Infrared spectrum of Comet Halley taken on 31 March 1986 by D. T. Wickramasinghe and D. A. Allen using the Anglo-Australian Telescope, shown as points. The flux is plotted on an arbitrary scale. The solid curve is a prediction for the *E. coli* bacterium at a single temperature (47°C); the dashed curve is for a spread of temperatures.

ishment of most astronomers, Comet Halley was still violently active in the cold depths of space half-way between the orbits of Saturn and Uranus. This observation alone is sufficient to dispose of the 'dirty snowball' model of comets, for snowballs do not explode in the cold depths of space, dirty or otherwise.

Before concluding this chapter it is necessary to say a little about comets in general. Most have orbits which are highly elongated. At each orbital revolution a typical comet comes close to the Sun only for a brief period of a few months. In this sense the Earth is also 'close' to the Sun. When a comet is at its nearest to the Sun, at a point known as 'perihelion', it is usually somewhere between the orbits of the planets Mercury and Mars. Cometary orbits are in general so elongated that most comets at their greatest distance from the Sun, at a point called 'aphelion', lie far beyond the orbits of the most remote planets, Neptune and Pluto. At these great distances they move slowly, so that orbital revolution periods are long, ranging from hundreds of years to tens of thousands of years.

But as always there are exceptions. Comet Halley is itself something of an exception, because it scarcely goes beyond the orbit of Neptune, whereas most comets go out much further. Even so, the orbit of Comet Halley is quite elongated, although not nearly as elongated as for most comets. Nevertheless, there are comets which stay closer to the Sun than Comet Halley does. Indeed, there are some which spend the whole of their time in the general region of the Earth and the other inner planets. All these short-period comets, as they are called, eject material as they go around the Sun, with the consequence that the Earth is perpetually embedded in a halo of material from short-period comets, material which forms a cloud occupying the inner regions of the Solar System, a cloud which does not recede to great distances with much of it lost into interstellar space, as is the fate of material ejected from the majority of comets.

Figure 4.6 shows the orbits of the innermost short-period comets, projected onto the plane of the Earth's orbit, the projections including orbits of high inclination. The three dashed circles mark the orbits of the Earth, Mars and Jupiter. Material ejected from a particular comet follows a distribution of orbits that, while varying somewhat, is generally like the orbit of the parent comet. Hence we have to think of ejected material from short-period comets forming a cloud with a multiplicity of orbits like that of Figure 4.6, which is clearly a complex situation.

Table 4.1 lists comets with orbital periods of less than 100 years. The unit of distance used in the table is known as the astronomical unit, abbreviated as AU; it is the Earth's mean distance from the Sun,

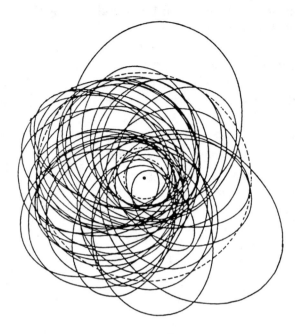

Figure 4.6 The orbits of short-period comets lie mostly in the region between Mars and Jupiter. This is the graveyard of the comets. (From N. B. Richter, *The Nature of Comets*, Methuen, 1963.)

about 150 million kilometres. The table includes the comets whose orbits are shown in Figure 4.6. Cometary orbits are susceptible to change by gravitational perturbation, particularly those of comets whose aphelion distance is close to the mean radius of Jupiter's orbit, which is 5.2 astronomical units. The values given are for epochs close to the year 1970. It will be seen that Comet Halley is at the extreme long end of this class of 'short-period' comets.

The problems to be considered and investigated in this book are the following. If material of biological origin – bacteria, viruses, protozoa, and perhaps still more complex structures – is being ejected from comets, how would this material interact with the Earth? What would be its effect on the evolution of terrestrial life? Could a whole range of phenomena, from the origins of life to evolution, as well as biomedical effects, be explained in this way? Would it explain the extinction of the dinosaurs?

Table 4.1 COMETS WITH ORBITAL PERIODS OF LESS THAN 100 YEARS.[a]

Name of comet	Period (years)	Perihelion	Aphelion
Encke	3.30	0.339	4.10
Grigg–Skjellerup	5.12	1.001	4.94
Honda–Mrkos–Pajdusaková	5.22	0.559	5.46
Tempel 2	5.276	1.364	4.68
Neujmin 2	5.43	1.338	4.84
Brorsen	5.46	0.590	5.61
Tuttle–Giacobini–Kresák	5.49	1.123	5.10
Tempel 1	5.50	1.497	4.73
Tempel–Swift	5.68	1.153	5.22
D'Arrest	6.23	1.167	5.61
Du Toit–Neujmin–Delporte	6.31	1.677	5.15
De Vico–Swipe	6.31	1.624	5.20
Pons–Winnecke	6.34	1.247	5.61
Giacobini–Zinner	6.41	0.934	5.97
Kopff	6.42	1.567	5.34
Forbes	6.42	1.545	5.37
Schwassmann–Wachmann 2	6.52	2.147	4.83
Wolf–Harrington	6.55	1.622	5.38
Biela	6.62	0.861	6.19
Tsuchinshan 1	6.64	1.493	5.57
Wirtanen	6.65	1.612	5.46
Perrine–Mrkos	6.72	1.272	5.85
Brooks 2	6.72	1.763	5.36
Reinmuth 2	6.73	1.942	5.19
Johnson	6.77	2.200	4.96
Tsuchinshan 2	6.80	1.775	5.40
Harrington	6.80	1.582	5.60
Arend–Rigaux	6.84	1.444	5.76
Finlay	6.90	1.080	6.17
Borrelly	6.99	1.447	5.87
Holmes	7.05	2.157	5.20
Daniel	7.09	1.662	5.72
Harrington–Abell	7.19	1.773	5.68
Shajn–Schaldach	7.27	2.227	5.28
Faye	7.41	1.616	5.98

Table 4.1 (cont.)

Name of comet	Period (years)	Perihelion	Aphelion
Ashbrook–Jackson	7.43	2.285	5.33
Whipple	7.47	2.480	5.16
Reinmuth 1	7.60	1.983	5.75
Arend	7.76	1.822	6.02
Oterma	7.88	3.388	4.53
Schaumasse	8.18	1.196	6.92
Jackson–Neujmin	8.39	1.428	6.83
Wolf	8.43	2.506	5.78
Comas Solá	8.55	1.769	6.59
Kearns–Kwee	9.01	2.229	6.43
Neujmin 3	10.95	2.032	7.83
Gale	10.99	1.183	8.70
Väisälä 1	11.28	1.866	8.19
Slaughter–Burnham	11.62	2.543	7.72
Van Biesbroeck	12.41	2.410	8.31
Tuttle	13.77	1.023	10.46
Schwassmann–Wachmann 1	16.10	5.538	7.21
Neujmin 1	17.93	1.543	12.16
Crommelin	27.87	0.743	17.64
Tempel–Tuttle	32.91	0.982	19.56
Stephan–Oterma	38.84	1.595	21.34
Westphal	61.88	1.254	30.03
Brorsen–Metcalf	69.06	0.485	33.18
Olbers	69.47	1.179	32.62
Pons–Brooks	70.98	0.774	33.51
Halley	76.09	0.587	35.33

[a] Not all these comets are still intact; some have disintegrated, such as Comet Biela, but their dust and debris could still be in orbit.

Source: B. G. Marsden, Catalogue of Cometary Orbits, Smithsonian Astrophysical Observatory, Cambridge, Massachusetts, 1972.

CHAPTER FIVE

The unearthly properties of plants and animals

The properties of plants and animals are determined by their genetic structures, which consist of a large number of individual units, genes, that in relatively simple organisms number a few thousand but in higher plants and animals appear to exceed a hundred thousand in total. A useful modern analogy is to think of the whole genetic structure as a computer program, with each individual gene acting as a subroutine within the main program, a subroutine for producing some particular biochemical substance that is necessary for the functioning of the organism.

The big problem in 'natural history', as it used to be called, is to understand how the living organisms in the world around us came to be the way they are. The answer of nineteenth-century biology was an early application of what in physics is known as feedback. Feedback is a process in which some property or other becomes accentuated through its own action. A species with slightly differing genetic structures among its members will consist of individuals having correspondingly differing physical properties, slight differences of size for example. Those properties which best permit the particular individuals possessing them to survive and reproduce their own genetic variants will increase from generation to generation more in proportion than other individuals with less beneficial genetic structures. The relative proportions of the different initial genetic variants will also change as time goes on. According to nineteenth-century biology, translated with little change into the twentieth century, all of the rich profusion of plants and animals is to be attributed to this process. One of the earliest clear statements of the feedback idea was given in 1831 by Patrick Matthew, who coined the words 'natural process of selection' to describe it, a name that was intended to distinguish selection in nature from the selection prac-tised artificially, for example by horticulturalists and stockmen. Thus Patrick Matthew wrote in 1831: –

From the unremitting operation of this law (the natural process of selection) acting in concert with the tendency which the progeny have to take the particular quality of their parents, a considerable uniformity of figure, colour, and character is induced, constituting species; the breed gradually acquiring the very best possible adaptation of these to its condition which it is susceptible of, and when alteration of circumstances occurs, thus changing in character to suit these as far as its nature is susceptible of change.

This statement left open the critical question of just how big the change of character might be that a 'breed' was 'susceptible of'.

From his writings, Matthew evidently believed that changes in species much larger than those produced by artificial selection by horticulturalists and stockmen could occur in nature, and in 1855, almost a quarter of a century later, it was shown by Alfred Russel Wallace that this opinion was correct. Even so, the work of 1855 still fell a long way short of demonstrating how the whole ensemble of plants and animals came into being. Wallace's paper on the subject was confined to the so-called Sarawak law, written from Sarawak on the island of Borneo where Wallace was at the time earning his living as a collector of plants and animals: 'Every species has come into existence coincident both in time and space with a pre-existing closely allied species.'

In a critical second paper written in February 1858, Wallace went further. He showed how, by applying the natural process of selection, it was possible to suggest an explanation of the origin of, not so much plants and animals themselves, as of the scheme by which biologists classify living organisms. He showed how it would be possible for varieties of a species to develop into distinct species, for species themselves to divide so as to form genera, genera to form families, and perhaps even further to still higher taxonomic categories. Already in 1855, Wallace had used the analogy of a branching tree to describe such a process, and in 1858 he gave reasons for thinking that evolution might really have happened like a branching tree, a main trunk giving rise to a few major branches, then each major branch giving rise to smaller branches, and so on eventually to the twigs and shoots that presently form the outer envelope of the tree.

In 1859 Charles Darwin published a major work of 160,000 words under the title *On the Origin of Species by Means of Natural Selection, or the Preservation of Favoured Races in the Struggle for Life*. While claiming extreme caution in his presentation, Darwin in fact did his utmost to convince his readers that all of life was to be explained by a combination of the feedback process of Patrick Matthew with Wallace's process of divergence from varieties to species, species to genera, and so on. It was claimed by Darwin and his supporters that over many years he had kept similar ideas locked away in his escritoire. This may have been so, but there is no really hard evidence to support such a view.

From a logical point of view, Charles Lyell raised what was a serious and valid objection to the *Origin of Species*. Lyell's main life's work had been to demonstrate the correctness of the principle of uniformity in geology, first announced by James Hutton towards the end of the eighteenth century, according to which the processes now at work on and inside the Earth have been operating in the same general way throughout geological history. It followed that, although the environment in which life operates may be changing perpetually in its fine detail, the overall environment has remained broadly the same during the time interval of about 500 million years over which life has changed from comparatively simple beginnings, from a neurological point of view, to its highly complex present-day forms. If species were always optimized to the maximum extent they were 'susceptible of', as Patrick Matthew had put it, how could this measure of change have come about with respect to a broadly unchanging environment? This was a question that Darwin and his followers dealt with by the device of ignoring it. What Lyell's question really demonstrated was that new genetic material must have become operative in some way within the terrestrial ensemble of plants and animals. Otherwise the ensemble would optimize itself to the environment, only fluctuating in comparatively minor ranges as the environment fluctuated. Such fluctuations could be sufficient to explain Wallace's observations of 1855, but they could not be sufficient to explain the major branchings in Wallace's tree of life.

There were plenty of objections of a more practical kind. It had to be accepted that evolution solely through Matthew's natural process of selection could never endow a plant or an animal with a property for which there had never been any need. Nor could the property come first in time and the usage second, because such an ordering would contradict the proper sequence of cause and effect. Yet there are easily noticed examples of both these impossible situations – impossible, that is, according to the claims of the *Origin of Species*. The eye, whether of a human or a gull, possesses superb compensations for spherical aberration, chromatic aberration, coma and astigmatism, to the extent that it is scarcely possible to match a biological eye with the best man-made device. It does not flout the proper sequence of cause and effect to suppose that a less well-compensated system might slowly evolve into a better-compensated system, but how could an eye, initially with such atrocious focus as to be useless, ever evolve by slow stages into an eye with a useful measure of focus? One can imagine an initial eye that would be useful simply as a light detector. But for such a simple detector to become also a focusing instrument capable of separating the visual background into discrete objects, it would be necessary to go from a condition of no-focus to one of useful focus all in one jump. This would seem to imply an injection of new genetic material from outside, all in one go, rather than a succession of small internal changes, no one of which could produce a step that was large enough to give the natural process of selection an edge to bite on.

It is well known in the physical sciences that it is often misleading to suppose objects with similar appearances, similar morphologies, to be causally related – because, of course, quite different causes can lead to similar appearances. The apparent sizes of the Sun and Moon as they appear in the sky are so nearly the same that in ancient times they would have been thought exactly the same, which must have appeared to demand a causal relationship when in fact the near-identity of apparent sizes is only coincidental. The forelimbs of reptiles and mammals have a common design consisting of a single major bone, going first to two bones and then through a 'wrist' to five digits at the extremity. This pentadactyl design was claimed by Darwin and his supporters to be indicative of a common origin in the pectoral fins of an ancestral fish. The hindlimbs of reptiles and mammals came, it was thought, from the pelvic fins of the ancestral fish. But why, then, if they do not come from the same fins, do the hindlimbs follow just the same design as the forelimbs, the same single bone going to two bones, an 'ankle' and five digits? It seems hard to argue that the design in question possessed such immense selective advantages as to exclude all other possibilities. The horse did not find five toes an advantage; quite the reverse: the horse found it an advantage to whittle the five toes down to only one. It seems better to argue that all vertebrates possess limbs of the same design because there was just one design available to them in the genetic material supplied from outside, one basic subroutine for producing limbs supplied to the terrestrial ensemble of animals. All would have to use the same basic system, subject to later modifications which each kind of animal developed for itself. This does not deny the usually claimed evolutionary picture. What it says is that an argument often advanced for the usual evolutionary picture is actually a *non sequitur* without any logical basis.

J. C. Willis was a distinguished botanist who, because he held posts first in Ceylon and then in Brazil, far outside the spheres of influence of learned societies in London, came to think for himself. Starting as a convinced Darwinian out of Cambridge, Willis came to see too many details that did not fit the Darwinian theory. In his book *The Course of Evolution by Divergent Mutation Rather than by Selection* (Cambridge University Press, 1940) Willis wrote:

Natural selection was, of course, essentially a theory of continuous adaptation to surrounding conditions.... A vast amount of energy was [therefore] put into the study of adaptation during the last quarter of the last century, and the imagination was pushed to the extreme limit to find some kind of adaptational value in even the less important features of plants. Unfortunately for the adaptationists and for the theory of natural selection no one was ever able to show that the important morphological features of plants, which showed so conspicuously in the characters that marked families, tribes, genera and most often also the species, had any adaptational value whatever, and the higher that one went in the scale, from species upwards, the more difficult was it to find such a value.

To give an example, as one goes along the stem of a plant, leaves may either alternate (left, right, left, right . . .) or occur in pairs. When in pairs they are exactly opposite. What would be the adaptational value of exactly opposite, Willis asks. Why not nearly opposite? Surely nearly opposite would have served the purpose of survival just as well as exactly opposite. If just two genetic subroutines for arranging leaves on stems have been distributed among plants, which have adopted one or the other more or less at random, Willis's remarks would be readily understandable.

Alfred Russel Wallace, who had done perhaps more than anyone else to support the concept of evolution by natural selection, came eventually to the conclusion that, while evolution through internally generated changes acted upon by selection works for some of the properties of plants and animals, for other properties it does not. Whereas for Willis it was mathematical patterns among flowers that seemed important, for Wallace is was mathematical patterns in the human head:

The law of Natural Selection or the survival of the fittest is, as its name implies, a rigid law, which acts by the life or death of the individuals submitted to its action. From its very nature it can act only on useful or hurtful characteristics, eliminating the latter and keeping up the former to a fairly general level of efficiency. Hence it necessarily follows that the characters developed by its means will be present in all the individuals of a species, and, though varying, will not vary very widely from a common standard. . . . In the speed of running, in bodily strength, in skill with weapons, in acuteness of vision, or in power of following a trail, all native peoples are fairly proficient, and the differences of endowment do not exceed the usual limits of variation in animals. So, in animal instinct or intelligence, we find the same general level of development. Every wren makes a fairly good nest like its fellows; even a fox has an average amount of the sagacity of its race; while all the higher birds and mammals have the necessary affections and instincts needful for the protection and bringing-up of their offspring.

But in specially developed faculties of civilised man the case is very different. They exist only in a small proportion of individuals, while the difference of capacity between these favoured individuals and the average of mankind is enormous. Taking first the mathematical faculty, probably fewer than one in a hundred really possess it, the great bulk of the population having no natural ability for the study, or feeling the slightest interest in it. And if we attempt to measure the amount of variation in the faculty itself between a first-class mathematician and the ordinary run of people who find any kind of calculation confusing and altogether devoid of interest, it is probable that the former could not be estimated at less than a hundred times the latter, and perhaps a thousand times would more nearly measure the difference between them.

The artistic faculty appears to agree pretty closely with the mathematical in its frequency. The boys and girls who, going beyond the mere conventional designs of children, draw what they see, not what they know to be the shape of things; who naturally sketch in perspective, because it is thus they see objects; who see, and represent in their sketches, the light and shade as well as the mere outlines of objects; and who can draw recognisable sketches of every one they know; are certainly very few compared with those who are totally incapable of anything of the kind. From some inquiries I have made in schools, and from my own observation, I believe that those who are endowed with this natural artistic talent do not exceed, even if they come up to, one per cent of the whole population. The variations in the amount of artistic faculty are certainly very great, even if we do not take the extremes. The gradations of power between the ordinary man or woman 'who does not draw', and whose attempts at representing any object, animate or inanimate, would be laughable, and the average good artist who, with a few bold strokes, can produce a recognisable and even effective sketch of a landscape, a street, or an animal, are very numerous; and we can hardly measure the difference between them at less than fifty or a hundred fold.

The musical faculty is undoubtedly, in its lower forms, less uncommon than either of the preceding but it still differs essentially from the necessary or useful faculties in that it is almost entirely wanting in one-half even of civilised men. For every person who draws, as it were instinctively, there are probably five or ten who sing or play without having been taught and from mere innate love and perception of melody and harmony. On the other hand, there are probably about as many who seem absolutely deficient in musical perception, who take little pleasure in it, who cannot perceive discords or remember tunes, and who could not learn to sing or play with any amount of study. The gradations, too, are here quite as great as in mathematics or pictorial art, and the special faculty of the great musical composer must be reckoned many hundreds or perhaps thousands of times greater than that of the ordinary 'unmusical' person . . .

We have thus shown, by two distinct lines of argument, that faculties are developed in civilised man which, both in their mode of origin, their function, and their variations, are altogether distinct from those other characters and faculties which are essential to him, and which have been brought to their actual state of efficiency by the necessities of his existence. And besides the three which have been specially referred to, there are others which evidently belong to the same class. Such is the metaphysical faculty, which enables us to form abstract conceptions of a kind the most remote from all practical applications, to discuss the ultimate causes of things, the nature and qualities of matter, motion, and force, of space and time, of cause and effect, of will and conscience. Speculations on these abstract and difficult questions are impossible to primitive peoples, who seem to have no mental faculty enabling them to grasp the essential ideas or conceptions; yet whenever any race attains civilisation, and comprises a body of people who whether as priests or philosophers, are relieved from the necessity of labour or of taking an active part in war or government, the metaphysical faculty appears to spring suddenly into existence, although, like the other faculties we have referred to, it is always confined to a very limited proportion of the population. (A. R. Wallace, *Contributions to the Theory of Natural Selection*, Macmillan, 1875, Chap. 10)

What Wallace noticed in these examples was an inversion of the expected relation of cause and effect, properties already possessed by the human brain before they had any possibility of application, and therefore any possibility of being preferred by natural selection. The properties were present already, waiting for the moment when they could profitably emerge, as if subroutines had been acquired but not yet come into general use in the aid of the main computer program. Wallace made the important point that such causally inverted properties appear only sporadically in a small proportion of the population, as if only in a small minority had the new subroutines managed to emerge in an accurately working condition. We can view this sporadically appearing small minority as mutants who come to nothing so long as their unusual talents remain irrelevant to survival. Each generation will then have its tiny number of mutants who come and go without any general change occurring in the genetic structure of a species. But let circumstances change so that such a mutant property becomes critical for survival, and selection will then operate to increase the minority possessing it, eventually leading to a property which began as a rarity becoming the norm.

Because the examples he gave all involved what might be considered to be higher abilities of the mind, Wallace imagined that some guiding effect of a specifically spiritual kind must be involved, as if evolution takes place by tooth and claw at lower levels but by spiritual guidance at higher levels. Yet just the same concepts apply throughout evolution, in Willis's examples from botany as well as Wallace's examples from mathematics and the arts. Indeed, to make sense of the title of Willis's book one must interpret his term 'divergent mutation' as meaning change through a major addition of new genetic material from outside a species, new subroutine(s) in our analogy.

In Chapter 3 we encountered properties that would be without proper cause if they were considered indigenous to the Earth, namely the uncanny ability of microorganisms to withstand immense doses of what, to us, would be exceedingly damaging radiation. From the ability of microorganisms to cope with conditions comparable to those inside a man-made nuclear reactor, and from their ability to cope with high concentrations of heavy radioactive nuclides such as the isotopes of americium and plutonium, it seems clear that the lower forms of life did not evolve upon the Earth, where no radiation-intense environment has existed since an atmosphere was acquired at an early stage in the history of our planet. Microorganisms possess properties that are unearthly, as we shall emphasize still more strongly in the next chapter. This is perhaps not so much of a surprise as the fact that, according to Willis, plants also possess properties that are best explained as unearthly, while Wallace's argument, given in detail above, even suggests that the most outstanding abilities of man are hardly to be understood in any other way than as being unearthly in their origin. The source of the wonderful adagio which Beethoven wrote in the second of his Opus 59 quartets, after gazing at the night sky for a long while, is perhaps then not so difficult to understand.

CHAPTER SIX

The beginnings of panspermia

We were led to our ideas on the cosmic nature of life by the astronomical considerations set out in Chapters 3 and 4, independently of historical considerations. We were aware of a theory going by the rather unattractive name of 'panspermia', against which the elder author had felt a measure of prejudice in his earlier years. When to our surprise we had been pulled by astronomical facts in the direction of life as a cosmic phenomenon, against initial prejudices, we became interested in what had been argued concerning panspermia in earlier decades and centuries.

There is a sense in which the ancient Greeks may be said to have thought of almost everything, but in another sense one can say that up to Archimedes the Greeks actually discovered rather little. Even though their perceptions were at times far-reaching, as in the atomic theory of Democritus (*c.*460 BC–*c.*370 BC), and a unity of being conceived of by Parmenides (*c.*500 BC) qualifying perhaps as the first-known tentative beginning of the panspermia theory, little in the way of certain knowledge was ever discovered. Conceiving of an idea is not the same as discovery, even if the idea subsequently turns out to be true. One may strongly suspect that an idea is true, but unless one can be certain about it other possibilities must still be kept in mind.

And as one idea leads to another, uncertainties tend to proliferate – like Wallace's tree of life, diverging more and more as one attempts to progress along a chain of pure reason. The only valid prescription for cutting down such an ever-growing tree of complexity is through observation or experiment, and the latter was generally not available to the Greeks in pre-Archimedean times. An invalid recipe for cutting down the trees of complexity in our lines of reasoning (one practised widely in all societies and at all times) is to cut away masses of branches through arbitrary precept, by convention, fashion or dogma. Whenever the brain becomes overwhelmed by growing complexity, the impulse is to simplify by excluding possibilities which should not be excluded, and it is in this impulse to seek relief from overcomplexity that lie most of the mistakes made by scientists and society.

It is safe to say that, were it not for observation and experiment permitting wrong alternatives to be dispensed with, every society would very quickly go seriously astray. The first relatively modern experiment relevant to the topic of this chapter was carried out in 1668 by the Italian physician Francesco Redi. He divided a number of flasks containing various meats into two sets, one set sealed from the air and the other open to the air. Although in all cases the meats putrified, it was only in those that were open, thereby permitting flies to enter, that maggots were found. This properly controlled experiment dealt a severe blow to the theory of spontaneous generation, according to which life was supposed to appear under appropriate conditions out of suitable inorganic material, as for instance Aristotle (384–322 BC) thought that fireflies emerge from a mixture of warm earth and morning dew, a view curiously similar to that of the organic soup story in Chapter 3. By the second half of the eighteenth century the idea that many processes we observe around us, the decay of plant material for example, and even epidemics of disease, are caused by small units of life had begun to be discussed, presumably as an outcome of microscopic observations which showed the existence of life-forms down to the limits of resolution of available instruments, about one-hundredth of a millimetre. Such microorganisms were then referred to collectively as 'germs'. Nobody then had any idea, however, of the existence of viruses, which did not become known until the late nineteenth century, and indeed it was not until 1915 that the real study of viruses began.

It seems to have been the Abbé Lazzaro Spallanzani (1729–99) who first wrote of germs as being generally distributed in the atmosphere, and it seems to have been from Spallanzani that the name panspermia has been adopted (*Opuscles de Physique, animale et végétale, Pavie*, 1787, Vol. I, p. 230). Nowadays, the term panspermia is taken to mean the cosmic distribution of microorganisms, whereas to begin with it meant germs distributed everywhere terrestrially. This early usage has of course turned out to be correct, as we think the extended cosmic usage will also be.

On 21 January 1870 the physicist John Tyndall gave a Friday evening discourse at the Royal Institution, London, in which he reported the presence everywhere in the atmosphere of small organic particles. This was a matter of experiment and could not be denied by critics of Tyndall's further speculation that the organic particles might contain living germs, and perhaps it was through breathing germs that epidemics of disease were spread. The principal critic was an anonymous writer in the weekly science magazine *Nature*, which had just begun to be published. The writer was evidently a strong supporter of Darwin, propaganda for whom seems to have been the main objective of the magazine, at any rate in its early days. Modern biologists may care to read the article 'The atmospheric-germ theory' published in the issue of *Nature* for Thursday, 3 February 1870, and note how many catastrophic mistakes it contains. Tyndall is criticized for assuming the germ theory of disease to be correct, and even Pasteur's work on fermentation and on silkworm disease is thrown into doubt: 'This was the doctrine [the widespread existence of microorganisms] of which M. Pasteur first attempted the experimental verification. How far he succeeded in the attempt is another question.'

What Darwinians could see, even as early as 1870, was that if microscopic units of life existed outside ordinary plants and animals, there was the possibility that changes had been induced in plants and animals by invasion from without. Evolution might then become more a question of invasion than of mutation occurring internally, in which case Darwin's cherished precept, *natura non facit saltum* (nature does not go in jumps) would be in danger. In the interest of preserving their dogmas, the early Darwinians were evidently prepared to deny bacteriology.

Even wilder than Tyndall, according to *Nature*, were those essentially insane individuals who thought that units of life might exist, not just terrestrially, but cosmically. Unfortunately for *Nature*, among the essentially insane individuals were some very notable scientists including Helmholtz in Germany and Lord Kelvin in Britain. Kelvin actually made the question of cosmic life a principal topic in his presidential address to the British Association in 1881. There has thus been a long history of opposition by physical scientists to the insistence of biologists, particularly Darwinians, that life is a closed system confined to the Earth. The opposition included internationally famous names, yet they did not make much impact with their views, and the Darwinians managed to clear the field to their own advantage, despite a whole series of errors just as serious as the denial of bacteriology and of the germ theory of diseases. The reason is partly that, whereas the opposition advanced its case as an intellectual argument, the Darwinians advanced theirs by incessant propaganda and by infiltrating the education system. But the larger part of the answer lies in the methodology of science. To be attractive to scientists in general, a theory must offer action, it must suggest something to be done next, a way to proceed, a way to make progress. The Darwinians made offers in plenty, whereas the supporters of panspermia were stumped as to what might be done to test and develop their views, because all those observations and experiments discussed above in Chapters 1 to 4 lay a century beyond the techniques which could be deployed in the latter half of the nineteenth century.

The fossil record showed that the animals of the past were often very different from those of today, yet it revealed nothing like the branching tree of life, which it should have done according to the Darwinian theory. This failure to match the predictions of the theory was excused by Darwin on the ground that the fossil record was grossly incomplete, a view strongly contested by Adam Sedgwick, Professor of Geology at Cambridge. The ensuing debate set up a practical objective, namely to examine fossils in hitherto unexplored rock sequences all over the world with a view to obtaining a much more complete record, a record sufficiently detailed to show at least some of the major connections of the branching tree predicted by the theory. Here was an explicit goal.

Rather quickly, a sequence of fossil horses dating from about fifty million years ago was uncovered, and was discussed in great detail, first by Vladimir Kovalevsky and then by Othniel C. Marsh. It was established that the horse had grown from the dimensions of a medium-sized dog to its present size, and that as it had done so over the interval of fifty million years, four toes initially at the front and three toes with a vestigial toe at the back had been whittled down to only a single toe at the extremity of each limb.

What these discoveries actually showed was very different from what was claimed, however. The discoveries showed that the horse had indeed evolved in the sense that it had changed appreciably, but this did nothing towards establishing the major branchings of the tree of life. It only showed that a particular kind of creature changed into a similar kind of creature, which was not really a new discovery at all. Indeed, fossil three-toed horses had been known from about 1850. Yet the discoveries were represented to the public as 'proof' of Darwin's theory, whereas they scarcely touched the question of whether the Darwinians were correct or not. The discoveries would still have permitted evolution in considerable jumps, whereas Darwin required the changes to occur by almost imperceptible degrees. Claims of imperceptible degrees were made by Marsh, but his claims are considered doubtful nowadays.

According to the Darwinians, every property of a plant or animal should be explicable as an adaptation to the environment, past or present. The long neck of the giraffe is the classic example of an adaptation, but this of course was long pre-Darwinian – it had already been discussed by Lamarck early in the nineteenth century. In the words of J. C. Willis:

A vast amount of energy was put into the study of adaptation during the last quarter of the last century. . . . Unfortunately for the adaptationists and for the theory of natural selection no one was ever able to show that the important features of plants . . . had any adaptational value whatever . . .

But at least the vast expenditure of energy noted by Willis gave botanists something to do, keeping them busy, if unprofitably, just as hunters for the fossil tree of life have been kept unprofitably busy to the present day.

With the coming of Mendelian genetics early in the present century, yet another hare was started. It was a mathematical hare, and so could be used to confuse the many people who find mathematics confusing. A few words of explanation may be useful. The positive properties possessed by a species arise from its genes, of which there are a large number. Provided a species has a sufficiently large membership, individuals lacking a particular property will arise in every generation because the process in which genes are copied from one generation to the next is not quite perfect. If a positive property is important to survival in the environment of the time, then the rare individuals who are unfortunate enough to be born with the property defective will be selected against, and their mis-copied genetic structure will not survive. It may happen, however, that an environmental change will make what was previously a positive property with an advantage into a disadvantage, in which case the rare individuals who are born with the property defective will be selected favourably, and their proportion in the community will increase. The process of selection continuing over a sufficient number of generations eventually produces a species for which the original positive property has been removed. In the sense that initially positive properties can be removed should changed circumstances warrant it, 'Darwin's theory' works. That is to say, so far as destruction is concerned it works, a result that can be demonstrated by precise mathematics.

Every member of a species that has lost some previous positive property, as for instance humans have lost the ability to grow fur all over the body, possesses a gene or genes very close to being in an operative condition, wrong by only a minimal amount. Should the environment shift back to what it was before, so that the positive property becomes an advantage again, might there be, among the many members of a species, a few for whom a copying error has the effect of correcting the previous mistake? Provided the species has a large enough membership, permitting many very small chances of such a correction occurring to be added together to give an appreciable total (like adding 2p for every member of the British population to give £1,000,000), this does indeed happen. Advantageous natural selection then operates to increase the progeny of individuals with the corrected gene, and eventually the situation returns to what it was in the first place.

The terrestrial environment fluctuates constantly, and the many species constantly jostling together for advantage, sometimes individual against individual, sometimes variety against variety, sometimes species against species, are themselves fluctuating genetically in response to the environment in a perpetually changing kaleidoscope. It was this process that Alfred Russel Wallace observed in such detail during his expeditions in the Amazon and in the Dutch East Indies, and which led him to exclaim in amazement at the richness of detail of the natural world. These were the steps that led Wallace to the ideas discussed in the previous chapter.

What cannot be done in 'Darwin's theory' is to find entirely new positive properties. To give a simple example: suppose a plant or animal possessed a gene which permitted it to generate a blue colour when operative, but which led to an indefinite grey when inoperative. Changes of the environment alternating between favouring blue and favouring grey could produce a situation in which the gene oscillated between working and not working. The plant or animal could not produce internally a modified gene that generates colours other than blue or grey. The organism could not become red if the gene for producing a red colour was not present in the first place. It is because species cannot produce entirely new properties by processes internal to themselves that they cannot adapt outside their initial potential. Species are thus locked into bands of possible variation, whose widths will be a topic for later discussion.

According to the usual scientific lore, Darwin is supposed to have had the first original perceptions of his theory in the late 1830s, following his return from the voyage of H.M.S. *Beagle*, perceptions that gradually clarified over the two decades leading up to the publication of the *Origin of Species* in 1859. It will probably therefore come as a surprise to the reader that Edward Blyth wrote of the theory as early as in 1837, as follows:

I would briefly dispatch ['Darwin's theory'] as able writers have *often* taken the subject in hand ... [our italics]. Were self-adaptation through internal changes to prevail to any extent, we should in vain seek for those constant and invariable distinctions which are found in nature. Instead of a species becoming gradually less numerous where its habitat grades imperceptibly away, we should discover a corresponding gradation in its adaptations. . . . The common jay is diffused over a wide range of latitude, but is the same in Italy as in Sweden: this would not be if the jay were capable of adjusting to latitude or climate . . .

This makes the same point as the above résumé of the mathematical results of modern genetics. Species are capable by internal means alone of adaptation over only fairly narrow bands, bands too narrow to permit evolution according to the bold picture of a branching tree. To produce large distinctions extending to orders and classes, species must acquire new genetic properties from outside themselves, as for instance a species without the ability to produce a red colour could acquire a gene for producing red pigment from some other species already possessing it. Genes acquired from outside are likely in most cases to remain dormant for a while, stored as a piece of DNA and replicating with the usual genetic complement of the organism in question, but ready to burst out in some new direction at an appropriate time in the future. When this happens, the organism makes a sudden change which appears inexplicable according to the Darwinian theory, since the organism then acquires new properties that have not been processed by previous natural selection. The situation is like Wallace's discussion quoted in the previous chapter of the higher intellectual capacities of humans, with characteristics – even profound characteristics – present in a dormant condition ahead of their need. This apparent inversion of what according to the Darwinian theory is the expected sequence of cause and effect is discussed in more detail in a later chapter.

Now we can see why the early Darwinians looked upon panspermia as a danger to their position, and why the writer of the article in the issue of *Nature* for 3 February 1870 was even willing to sacrifice the latest developments in bacteriology to maintain the Darwinian momentum, which became not so much a scientific theory as a sociological movement. It was against the sociological aspects of Darwinism that even distinguished physicists like Lord Kelvin and

Hermann von Helmholtz were relatively powerless, especially as the sociological momentum was increased by bits of luck like the sequence of fossil horses, and by misrepresentation amounting even in some cases to deception. Nevertheless, the tension was building. As we shall see in the next chapter, the recoil could quite well have come early in the present century; if 'Darwin's theory' had not worked its way so strongly into the education system, this might well have happened. Instead, the inevitable confrontation has been postponed, with consequences that have now become explosive, through the accumulation of new ideas and facts. Some of these we considered in earlier chapters; others we shall look at in the chapters that follow.

CHAPTER SEVEN

The unearthly properties of microorganisms

What scientists judge to be the most likely explanations of the events we perceive in the world around us *should* depend only on the facts as they are presently known. But this is not so, or even nearly so. A great deal of what scientists currently believe to be true depends not so much on the facts as on the order in which the facts were discovered. Facts that would easily suffice to knock a theory on the head if they were known at the time the theory was first proposed, will hardly cause a ripple if discovered after the theory has become firmly established in the education system. If in 1859 the facts of bacteriology in particular and microbiology in general had been known, nobody would have taken the *Origin of Species* seriously.

Bacteria and other microorganisms are plainly not adapted to their environment as they should be if the Darwinian theory were correct. Species of microorganisms exist if the environment permits them to, with every indication of having pre-existed as we find them now, and of having simply fitted themselves into whatever environmental conditions there might be. Species replicating best under warm conditions are nevertheless found in Arctic waters, and vice versa. When human activities create new environmental conditions, new species of microorganisms appear that were not previously known, as if a wide range of organisms spanning an immense spectrum of environmental possibilities were constantly being rained upon the Earth from outside. Identical species of single-celled algae called diatoms, which apparently cannot exist at all under warm conditions and so should not be able to spread across the Earth's equatorial zone, are found in both the Arctic and the Antarctic, suggesting that they fell into both polar regions from space. Examples of hitherto unknown microbial species appearing in new man-made environments are common in modern industrial conditions, as for instance in tailings from mines of various types. In one remarkable case, in a modern sewage farm there appeared methane-producing bacteria thriving in a 4-to-1 mixture of free hydrogen to carbon dioxide, an optimum temperature of 65°C and the total absence of atmospheric oxygen.

The most striking aspects of microorganisms, however, are their unearthly properties, properties for which no environmental reason exists here on the Earth, and which should therefore never arise according to the Darwinian theory. The first such property was brought to light early in the present century by the Swedish chemist Svante Arrhenius. Arrhenius followed Kelvin and Helmholtz by interpreting the panspermia theory within a cosmic setting, rather than the terrestrial setting of the Abbé Spallanzani. If such a theory were correct, Arrhenius reasoned, it would be necessary for living cells to be able to survive great cold, because the depths of space remote from any star would be very cold, far more so than any environment on the Earth. So here at last was something which could actually be done in the laboratory to test the theory, since by the early years of the present century it had become possible to reach low enough temperatures, something which could not have been done thirty years earlier in the days of John Tyndall. In his book *Worlds in the Making* (New York and London, 1908), Arrhenius described what happened when the test was carried out:

In recent years experiments have been made in the Jenner Institute, in London, with spores of bacteria which were kept for twenty hours at a temperature of −252° [Celsius] in liquid hydrogen. Their germinating power was not destroyed thereby.

Professor Macfadyen has, indeed, gone still further. He has demonstrated that micro-organisms may be kept in liquid air (at − 200° [Celsius]) for six months without being deprived of their germinating power.

If this experiment had been done in 1870 it would almost surely have caused a sensation. In 1908 it scarcely caused a ripple, because by then, as a result of long-sustained propaganda, belief in 'Darwin's theory' had become almost as central to the education system as the laws of arithmetic. Likewise, there was hardly a ripple when the following result was reported in 1971. On 19 April 1967, the un-manned Surveyor 3 probe landed successfully on the Moon near the eastern edge of *Oceanus Procellarum*, the largest of the lunar 'seas'. On 20 November 1969, the TV camera carried on Surveyor 3 was retrieved by crew members of the Apollo 12 mission. On return to the Earth, the TV camera was examined in quarantine and was found to contain living bacteria of the species *Streptococcus mitis*. It appeared that the bacteria had survived two years of exposure to the lunar environment, at very low pressure and with repeated temperature fluctuations between a high comparable to the usual boiling point of water and a low of minus 150°C during the lunar night, a range far greater than anything experienced on Earth. The organisms survived because they had unearthly properties, which they could not possibly have had if they had been of terrestrial origin.

Once dogma has become established, people exposed to it become incapable of noticing even grossly discordant facts. What is done in such a situation is to invent supposed facts, phantom facts, to support the position. In the wake of the remarkable discovery that micro-organisms remain viable down to exceedingly low temperatures not much above absolute zero, the claim was made that microorganisms in space could not remain viable because of the damaging effect of ultraviolet radiation from high-temperature stars. This phantom claim became widely quoted without anybody troubling to consult a text-book on physics, which would immediately have shown that ultra-violet radiation is the easiest of all forms of radiation to exclude, only a little shielding material needing to lie between the source of the radiation and anything that might be sensitive to damage by it. Indeed, the interstellar dust is itself an excellent shielding agent. If the dust consists of bacteria, as earlier chapters suggested, the bacteria are self-shielding in the sense that, while those nearest to sources of ultraviolet radiation might well be inactivated or even charred, those more strategically placed, especially within denser interstellar clouds, would be safely shielded from serious damage.

More important, however, when one looks in detail at the behaviour of microorganisms after exposure to ultraviolet radiation, further unearthly properties come to light. Ultraviolet radiation does not so much kill microorganisms as inactivate them by shifting certain chemical bonds between bases contained in the genetic structures of the organisms. It was discovered in the late 1940s that this process of inactivation is actually reversible, and that microorganisms possess enzymes which in the presence of visible light have the effect of shifting the chemical bonds back to what they should properly be. Thus microorganisms are able to recover their viability after being temporarily inactivated by ultraviolet radiation, yet another unearthly property.

Some microorganisms, for example the flagellate *Bodo marina*, have very high powers of resistance to inactivation by ultraviolet radiation. These, it seems, differ from relatively susceptible organisms such as the bacterium *Escherichia coli* by possessing exceptionally effective enzymic repair systems. But most remarkably, even normally susceptible systems like *E. coli* can be induced to switch on repair systems that match those of the seemingly far more resistant organisms like *B. marina*. The experimental proof of this result is surely an outstanding demonstration of the existence of manifestly unearthly properties. It is possible to determine what dose of ultraviolet radiation will inactivate exactly half of a particular culture of *E. coli* exposed to it. Repetition of the same dose then inactivates half the bacteria which survived the first dose, and so on, like the decay of a radioactive material – but only for a while. Unlike radioactive material, which goes on halving indefinitely, the repeated halvings of the remaining viable fraction of bacteria eventually stops, a stage being reached after which comparatively few of the remaining bacteria become inactivated.

Experimenters found that saturation effects set in when the remaining viable bacteria numbered about one part in a thousand of the original total. The obvious thought was that one part in a thousand of the original culture happened to be an exceptionally radiation-resistant strain, present initially at low concentrations. If so, reculturing of the remaining residue should have produced an ultraviolet-resistant strain of *E. coli*. But this was not what happened. Reculturing from the remaining residue only re-established the original situation, half the recultured bacteria becoming inactivated by just the same radiation dose as before.

We interpret this result as demonstrating the ability of bacteria to learn by experience. Those bacteria which remained active after extended doses of radiation had managed to improve the efficiency of their repair system to cope with the continuing stress. When the stress was removed in reculturing, the repair system simply reverted to its normally much lower level of efficiency. Learning to cope with a stress not present in the natural terrestrial environment was most unearthly.

The position today with respect to testing the intrinsic Darwinian theory on the one hand and the extrinsic panspermia theory on the other is the opposite of what it was in 1870. Instead of it being difficult to find tests of the extrinsic theory, there is now a large body of facts which can be brought to bear on the extrinsic theory. Some of these facts have been considered in earlier chapters; more are to come. Instead of Darwin's theory being tested nowadays, the pretence is made that tests are not required because the theory is sufficiently well proven, whereas the truth of the matter is that, despite a veritable army of geologists examining rock sequences from all over the world, the fossil record is no nearer to proving 'Darwin's theory' than it was in the beginning. The mathematical theory of genetics is not favourable either; proof through the study of adaptations and morphologies is as illusive as ever; the organic-soup establishment is in a worse condition than when that particular idea originated in 1924; and the clear emergence of unearthly properties gives a disproof much stronger than any of the claimed proofs, all of which have turned out to be either logical *non sequiturs* or illusions.

Unfortunately for the panspermia theory, Svante Arrhenius handed a temporary victory to his opponents when in 1908 he wrote in the concluding paragraph of *Worlds in the Making*:

There is little probability, though, of our ever being able to demonstrate the correctness of [the panspermia theory] by an examination of seeds [microorganisms] falling down upon our Earth. For the number of germs which reach us from other worlds will be extremely limited – not more, perhaps, than a few within a year all over the Earth's surface; and those, moreover, will presumably strongly resemble the single celled spores with which the winds play in our atmosphere. It would be difficult, if not impossible, to prove the celestial origin of any such germs if they should be found ...

This was a counsel of despair. Scientific opinion does not take kindly to theories that are offered in an untestable form, which was how Arrhenius presented the panspermia theory. Fortunately, the theory outlined in Chapters 3 and 4 led to an entirely different picture of the arrival of microorganisms on the Earth. Figure 4.6 in Chapter 4 implies that the Earth is perpetually embedded in a halo of material evaporated from short-period comets. The amount of this material swept up annually by the Earth's atmosphere has been estimated from observations of meteors, and also from the observed density of the halo itself, to be about 1000 tonnes. If the material were made up largely of microorganisms, or even if a tolerable fraction were, the number of 'seeds' or 'germs' to reach us annually from 'other worlds' would be of the order of 10^{21}. This immense number is calculated for microorganisms consisting of bacteria and small protozoans. If an appreciable fraction of cometary material were viruses (as a strong measured ultraviolet component in the sunlight scattered by the zodiacal halo seems to suggest), the number of viruses could be considerably larger, say 10^{25}. The picture is therefore totally different from the one discussed by Arrhenius, as indeed were the discussions in Chapters 3 and 4. The basic idea is the same, but the *modus operandi* is quite different, changing the theory from being untestable in Arrhenius's form to overwhelmingly testable in the present form. If 10^{21} bacteria and 10^{25} viruses enter our atmosphere each year, their influence on the whole ensemble of terrestrial plants and animals can hardly be missed.

CHAPTER EIGHT

The entry of microorganisms into the Earth's atmosphere

The Earth moves at what from an everyday point of view is an extremely high speed with respect to the halo of cometary debris in which it is embedded, a speed with respect to a typical particle in its neighbourhood of about 10 kilometres per second, or 36,000 kilometres per hour. Even a hardy bacterium with its strong cell wall hitting a solid surface at so great a speed would be shattered, not just into its gross constituents like an insect hitting the windscreen of a fast-moving car, but into individual molecules and atoms. Micro-organisms in the local cometary debris would explode on hitting the surface of the Moon, but for the Earth the situation is different. Instead of their high speeds being checked almost instantaneously, as happens in hitting a solid surface, microorganisms entering the Earth's upper atmosphere would have their speeds checked much more slowly, because the gas density there is very low. In effect, by being slowed right down over 100 kilometres above the Earth's surface, the microorganisms would secure a soft landing, and not be destroyed like insects on a car windscreen.

Nevertheless, frictional heating caused by the impact of gas molecules, even in a low-density atmosphere, could present a hazard to the survival of such microorganisms. In two important ways, however, we can see immediately that the situation is favourable to survival. The flash heatings last for only about a second, and take place in gas of such low density that there is insufficient oxygen around for burning to occur. Even so, the question cannot be dismissed without careful investigation, because even without burning through oxidation, as in a normal fire, heated biomaterial can undergo internal chemical reactions that in a bacterium or virus could cause loss of viability. There could be an unacceptable measure of charring if chemical bondings are changed so as to drive off water molecules, for instance.

Heating depends on particle size, in such a way that the maximum temperatures attained by an incoming particle of specified speed depends approximately on the fourth root of its linear size. A particle the size of a pinhead entering the Earth's atmosphere at a speed of 10 kilometres per second would be heated to a maximum temperature of about 3000°C, sufficient for the particle to evaporate into a trail of hot gas, which because it is hot emits light as it cools. This is just what happens when we see meteors, flashes of light streaking across the sky on a clear dark night. Small particles about the size of a pinhead, meteoroids, are entering the Earth's atmosphere from outside and are evaporating due to atmospheric friction into trails of hot, luminous gas.

Fortunately for the theory, microorganisms are much smaller than a pinhead and do not become anything like as hot. A particle the size of a human blood cell would be momentarily heated to about 1000°C, viruses and typical bacteria to about 500°C. Could they survive such a short-term heating? This is exactly the kind of question that cannot be settled by arguing about it in the manner of the philosophers of ancient times. One must try it and see.

The following experiment was carried out by Dr Shirwan Al-Mufti at the University of Wales, College of Cardiff. Samples of a culture of *Escherichia coli* were placed in a number of glass tubes which were then sealed, leaving an amount of air inside the tubes that was similar to the amount that would be encountered during flash heating by a bacterium plunging into the atmosphere. Each of the tubes was inserted into a hot oven at a particular carefully measured temperature, which was varied during the experiment from 300 to 700°C.

The sheer mechanics of inserting a tube in an oven and then taking it out again took about 20 seconds, longer than the flash heating of a microorganism entering the atmosphere, thereby making the experiment a more severe test of survival.

After withdrawal from the furnace, each tube was broken open and its contents transferred to a nutrient broth. Subjective judgement on inspection of the charred samples exposed to the highest temperature, 700°C or thereabouts, would have given them little chance of successful growth. Yet in all cases up to the highest temperatures for which the furnace was accurately calibrated, growth occurred, eventually back to normality. Care was taken to exclude the possibility of contamination, although contamination was in any case excluded by the manner of growth. *E. coli* normally replicates by binary fission, each cell dividing to form two daughter cells. Growth following flash heating occurred in clusters, with a bacterial cell usually dividing to form more than two daughter cells, commonly a cluster of four. This is a known property to happen with many species of bacteria after they have been subjected to severe stress, and so provides a useful verification that growth has not been due to stray contaminant bacteria.

In addition to demonstrating that microorganisms could survive passage through the Earth's atmosphere, this experiment yielded a remarkable additional result. The higher the temperature to which a sample was exposed, the slower it grew in the nutrient broth. A sample exposed to 700°C grew about four times more slowly than normal samples from the initial culture. But a sample exposed first at 300°C and then at 700°C grew only about twice as slowly as a normal sample, showing that preheating to 300°C enabled the bacteria to withstand subsequent heating to 700°C significantly better than bacteria that were not preheated. As in the radiation experiments discussed in Chapter 7, the bacteria appeared to learn from a smaller stress how better to cope with a larger stress, yet another example of an unearthly property. Flash heating to 700°C is something that emphatically does not occur in the terrestrial environment. How then, according to the Darwinian theory could such a property ever have evolved? Taking a much broader view, the need for microorganisms moving at high speeds to make successful soft landings on bodies like planets and satellites possessing atmospheres may well have played a crucial role in the evolution of life on a cosmic scale.

The existence of not just one, but many unearthly properties – the more one looks for them the more one finds – reverses sharply the logic formerly used against the panspermia theory. Instead of the problem being survival in a space environment, a seemingly insuperable problem now confronts conventional theory, namely to explain how, according to Darwinism, microorganisms that are supposed never to have been outside the terrestrial environment could have acquired properties so remarkable and so profoundly suited to a space environment. From a logical point of view, the problem here for Darwinism is really the same inversion of cause and effect that was emphasized by Alfred Russel Wallace in connection with the mental qualities of humans (Chapter 5), the existence of properties which according to 'Darwin's theory' should not be there. The appearance of the same problem at both the lower and higher ends of the scale of complexity of living organisms points strongly to a fundamental deficiency of that theory, a deficiency much greater than Wallace suspected in the remarks quoted in Chapter 5.

The Earth's atmosphere can be thought of, for our purposes, as being divided into three parts: a lower region, the troposphere; a middle region, the stratosphere; and an upper region, the mesosphere. Microorganisms from space land in the mesosphere at a height of about 120 kilometres above the Earth's surface. Once landed, they would be brought down to the stratosphere by atmospheric movements, probably in a matter of a few days, since the gases in the mesosphere are constantly being vigorously stirred by solar heating. Ozone, which extends to the top of the stratosphere, gives protection against ultraviolet radiation from the Sun, while the gases of the mesosphere give protection against X-rays. Thus microorganisms reaching the stratosphere in a viable condition can be considered safe from further risk of radiation damage. Also, microorganisms landing in a polar region in winter would be entirely protected from the Sun, even while descending through the mesosphere.

The lower atmosphere, the troposphere, has an upper limit which varies from about 18 kilometres in the tropics, to 10 kilometres in temperate latitudes and 7 kilometres in polar regions. Small particles over the whole size range from viruses at the lower end to colonies of bacteria at the upper end descend comparatively quickly from the top of the troposphere to ground-level. In the troposphere, the temperature falls with increasing height, encouraging vertical air movements that carry water vapour upwards from the surface regions to the top of the troposphere. As the temperature falls with increasing height the water vapour becomes supersaturated, but the temperature is not usually so low that supersaturated water vapour condenses spontaneously into ice crystals. Ice requires something to condense around – a nucleus (in this sense meaning a small particle, not the nucleus of an atom). Small particles falling from the stratosphere above into the troposphere, and in particular microorganisms falling from above, would provide such nuclei around which much larger ice crystals could form. Because larger ice crystals are less impeded by air resistance than the original small nuclei, they fall much faster. As they descend into warmer air the ice crystals usually melt, and the resulting water droplets may either fall to the ground as rain, or only partially evaporate, with the resulting smaller droplets remaining suspended as a haze in the air. Normal precipitation rates are such that this process, often involving repeated cycles of condensation and evaporation of the ice crystals and water droplets, serves to wash out the troposphere of small particles in a timescale of a few weeks.

Instead of continuing to fall above the top of the troposphere, the temperature then rises with increasing height, from about minus 55°C at the top of the troposphere – the bottom of the stratosphere – to about plus 3°C at the top of the stratosphere, at an altitude of about 50 kilometres above ground-level. The physical reason for this temperature inversion, as it is called, is that ozone in the stratosphere absorbs solar ultraviolet radiation very strongly, thereby giving an energy input into the stratosphere. The physical effect of the temperature inversion is to inhibit greatly the generally free movement of air that occurs in the troposphere. Travellers by air will be familiar with the difference between the clarity of the lower stratosphere into which aircraft normally climb and the cloudy turbulent troposphere below. Free air movement in the stratosphere is limited to west-to-east movements along parallels of latitude of which the most violent are the jet streams. The effect of the free west-to-east movement is to produce a general uniformity with respect to longitude in the stratospheric distribution of small particles. If the Earth were smooth at its surface, we would therefore expect any incoming micro-organisms from space to arrive at ground-level at more or less the same times along a given parallel of latitude. But because the tropo-sphere has a marked dependence of height on latitude, we would not expect different latitudes to behave similarly except for particles larger than viruses and individual bacteria, particles that were large enough to fall rapidly without much regard to air resistance. Even for a given parallel of latitude, the fact that the Earth's surface is not smooth makes for marked differences in the times of descent of incoming particles. This is true particularly for descent upon regions of high relief, as in mountainous areas. An interesting case is for latitudes of about 30°N, along which the Himalayas project upwards through about half the height of the troposphere. The high peaks of this mountain range effectively introduce easy downward routes at the base of the stratosphere for the descent of incoming particles. We would thus expect floods of microorganisms to fall downwind of mountain ranges such as the Himalayas.

Considering now particles of various sizes, comparatively large particles such as bacterial colonies would fall rapidly everywhere over the Earth, because gravity pulling them downwards is more significant than air resistance. Individual bacteria fall through the lowest ten kilometres of the stratosphere at a rate of one or two centimetres a minute. Because there is more of the stratosphere through which such a particle must fall in high latitudes than in the tropics (the troposphere is higher in the tropics), a bacterium takes longer to reach ground-level in high latitudes, about two years compared with about a year in the tropics.

Air resistance is still more important for viruses. Thus a typical viral particle would take about 30 years to fall through the lowest ten kilometres of the stratosphere, if there were no vertical air movements at all in the stratosphere. Actually, although vertical mass movements of air in the stratosphere are feeble, there is sufficient stirring to allow the descent of small viruses. The physical cause of such stratospheric air movements is the equator-to-pole temperature difference, which powers a complex heat engine that operates more strongly the larger the temperature difference – that is, much more strongly in winter than in summer. Ozone measurements can be used to trace these mass movements of air in the stratosphere, and show a winter down-draft that is strongest over the latitude range 40°–60°. Taking advantage of this winter downdraft, individual viral particles arriving from space would tend to reach ground-level in temperate latitudes, so that any interaction they might have with terrestrial plants and animals would show most strongly there (once again, on the supposition that the Earth's surface is smooth). The exceptionally high mountains of the Himalayas, rearing up through much of the height of the troposphere, introduces a large perturbation, draining most of the viruses incident on the atmosphere at latitudes near 30°N, affecting, we might expect, the very large human populations of China and Southeast Asia.

A direct demonstration that the general winter downdraft in the stratosphere occurs most strongly over the latitude range 40°–60° was provided by the results of an experiment in which the radioactive isotope rhodium-102 was introduced into the atmosphere at a height of about 100 kilometres, and its subsequent descent to the bottom of the stratosphere was monitored. The results obtained are shown for three latitude ranges in Figure 8.1. The vertical axis gives the rhodium-102 count on a logarithmic scale, while the months at which the counts were made form the horizontal scale. The appearance of high counts between January and March in mid-latitudes is especially noteworthy.

We have seen how microorganisms are carried to ground-level inside ice crystals and water droplets. In trickles and streams and in ground water, they can reach into almost every nook and cranny of the Earth; surprisingly perhaps, they can even reach into the noses, mouths, snouts and lungs of animals. It is a matter of experience that we do not normally snuffle raindrops up into our nose or gulp them into our mouth. But a shower of rain does not end because all the water has fallen out of the atmosphere, it ends because falling droplets evaporate before they reach the ground. Droplets evaporating immediately in front of one's face would release viral particles into the air, ready to be breathed into the respiratory tract. It is therefore

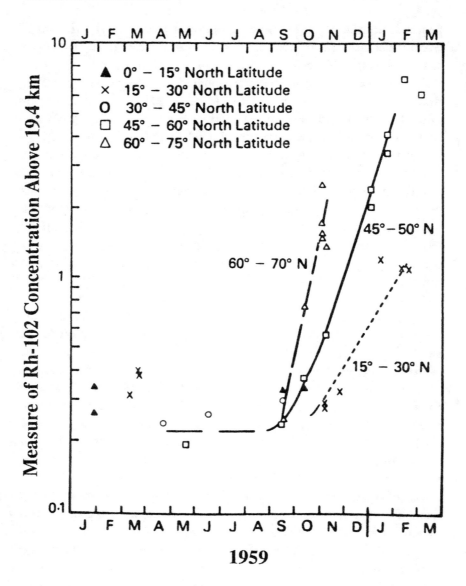

Figure 8.1 The fall-out of rhodium-102 at various latitude intervals from the HARDTACK atmospheric nuclear bomb exploded on 11 August 1958. (After M. I. Kalkstein, *Science*, 1962, **137**, 645.)

the end of a shower of rain that would lead to our breathing micro-organisms incident from space, and the details of such a process would be highly local and irregular.

The above discussion has been biased to suit the situation in northern temperate latitudes. In desert conditions other factors would be important. Precipitation in deserts tends to be one thing or the other, either heavy or absent, with little of the damp, drizzly weather of northern latitudes. Viruses falling from the atmosphere would mostly reach ground-level on rare occasions of heavy rainfall. Once on the ground they would stay there, instead of being washed to the sea in streams and rivers, ready to be lifted into the atmosphere again by winds. Windy periods with sandstorms would thus be the occasions on which microorganisms from space would most likely get into the respiratory tracts of humans and other animals. This expectation tallies well with experience of epidemic patterns in sub-Saharan Africa.

There is still another channel whereby viruses from space may succeed in entering our respiratory tracts. While most of the falling viruses to reach ground-level in regions other than deserts will be washed away by streams and rivers, some viral particles would remain suspended in the subsurface water, and some would accumulate in freshwater lakes. Evaporation provides a way in which water-embedded viruses and bacteria could subsequently be released into the atmosphere near ground-level, indoors from the domestic water supply at all times of the year, and outside mostly in spring and summer. A high-volume channel of this kind is evaporation from the leaves of trees, which is especially interesting because of the tendency of people to have trees near their houses, and because the evaporation process cools the air around the trees by the absorption of heat necessary to supply the latent heat of evaporation. The cool air, being denser in summer than the warm surrounding air, falls immediately to ground-level, thereby dumping any viruses it may contain on unsuspecting people living or picnicking in the shelter of the trees.

The biological system of a tree probably filters out most viruses, but a minority may well be expelled by both trees and foliage of all kinds out into the atmosphere, where they would be breathable by animals. Figure 8.2 shows the incidence of the human summer disease

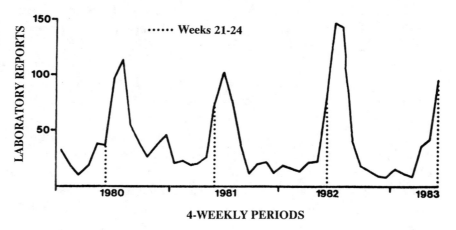

Figure 8.2 The incidence of parainfluenza type 3. (From *Communicable Disease Report 83/24*, Communicable Disease Surveillance Centre, London, 1983.)

of parainfluenza, a viral disease. Year after year in Britain, cases begin a steep rise at the end of April, attain a maximum in June, and fall essentially to zero in September, in correspondence with the annual growing cycle of plants. It is hard to imagine any other process that could give a cycle so repeated and so perfectly timed, although of course we have not yet proved that the causative virus comes from space. Proof requires an extended discussion that will occupy us in the next two chapters.

CHAPTER NINE

Consistency checks on the theory

Microorganisms of cometary origin will be incident on other bodies of the Solar System as well as the Earth, so that we can also look for indications of the correctness of the theory elsewhere in the Solar System. A great deal is known about the surface of the Moon, but unfortunately microorganisms could not land intact upon the Moon, because of the lack of any lunar atmosphere to provide a soft landing. Microorganisms hitting the surface of the Moon would be exploded into atoms and relatively simple molecules. The only feasible test of the theory that can be hoped for in the case of the Moon must therefore depend on gross elemental abundances (the relative amounts of the various chemical elements present), or on the presence in the lunar soil of relatively simple molecules of an organic nature which have managed to survive the high-speed impacts of their parent organisms, organisms derived from the halo of cometary organic material in which the Moon is embedded just as much as the Earth.

In the latter connection, small quantities of amino acids in samples of lunar soil have persistently been reported, while of gross elemental abundances, that of carbon seems the most interesting. Elemental abundances in the lunar soil are heavily dominated by oxygen, magnesium, aluminium, silicon and calcium, the elements that are dominant in terrestrial rocks, showing that lunar soil is mostly either ground-up rock or small rock-like particles which never became compacted. It is therefore curious that carbon, which is not a constituent of typical rocks, is present in lunar soil at a concentration of about one part in ten thousand. There is a diffuse wind of material blowing outwards all the time from the Sun, material containing carbon atoms, and it has been suggested that the carbon in the lunar soil may have become lodged there over long periods of time by this slight but steady rain of material from the Sun. If so, there would be no need to invoke a rain of microorganisms from cometary sources to supply the carbon. The issue turns on how long the solar wind is given for carbon to accumulate in the lunar surface layers – in other words, how deep the carbon goes below the immediate surface layers. Only if the depth is small could the solar wind supply sufficient carbon. Cores have been taken penetrating a metre or more into the soil, and carbon continues to be present in essentially unvarying concentration regardless of depth in such cores, showing that the carbon-containing surface layer is not extremely thin. This result pretty well rules out the solar-wind theory, unless one supposes that the top metre of lunar soil has lain there for 1000 million years or more, which seems doubtful in view of the following result from the Apollo 16 lunar mission.

The two largest craters in the vicinity of the landing site, in the lunar highlands near the crater Descartes, named North Ray Crater and South Ray Crater by the astronauts, were several metres deep and about a hundred metres in diameter. Debris thrown out when the craters were formed by the high-speed impact of objects probably about a metre in size was collected and brought back to Earth. Analysis of the debris showed the ages of both craters to be around 10 million years, which for events on the Moon is relatively recent. The far more numerous craters comparable in size to North and South Ray Craters which must have been formed in the Moon's earlier history have largely disappeared, apparently through a general turning-over of the lunar soil, termed 'gardening'. The gardening would need to be vigorous enough to fill in and smooth away depressions to depths of several metres, implying a gardening rate much faster than lunar scientists would prefer to suppose, but a rate hard we think to deny, a rate so relatively fast as probably to rule out the solar-wind hypothesis for the origin of carbon in the lunar soil.

If, on the other hand, one requires the carbon in the top few metres of lunar soil to have been supplied on a timescale of only 10 million years, consistent with the ages and sizes of North and South Ray Craters, the accumulation rate would be equivalent to the carbon contained in some tens of millions of bacteria taken to be incident each year on each square metre of the lunar surface, a rate satisfactorily consistent with the estimate of Chapter 7 for the whole Earth.

In 1976 two space probes, Vikings 1 and 2, were sent to Mars by NASA with experiments on board designed to test for the presence of microorganisms in the Martian soil. Mars possesses enough of an atmosphere to permit the soft landing of microorganisms, so on the present theory a positive result might have been obtained by the experiments, provided they were capable of detecting levels of concentration of microorganisms comparable to those found in comparatively barren soils on Earth, such as soils from the dry valleys of the Antarctic, where physical conditions approach most closely those on Mars. NASA apparently did not have the experiments on the Viking landers calibrated against Antarctic soils in advance of the missions, and this led to what has proved to be an unfortunate story.

In one experiment, a gas chromatograph and a mass spectrometer (GC/MS) were used to test for the presence of organic material of a kind normally associated with living systems, while another, the 'labelled release' (LR) experiment, was designed to test for biological activity of the type that occurs when microorganisms replicate. The LR experiment consisted basically of supplying a sample of Martian soil with a nutrient that contained radioactive carbon (carbon-14), then looking for the presence of radioactivity in any gas that was exuded by the sample as a consequence of biological activity. A control on the LR experiment was obtained by treating a second soil sample in a manner that experience in a terrestrial laboratory showed would sterilize soils such as those from Antarctic valleys.

The outcome was that in all cases the LR experiment gave positive results from unsterilized samples, but negative results from sterilized samples. The GC/MS experiment, on the other hand, was judged always to give negative results, and on this basis – one experiment positive, the other negative – NASA announced to the waiting world that no life had been found at particular sites on Mars, a statement quickly extended by commentators to the stronger form that there was no life at all on Mars. It was said that the LR experiment had given positive results because of the presence of some unexpected strong oxidizing agent, hydrogen peroxide perhaps, in the Martian soil. The designers of the LR experiment, Gilbert V. Levin and Patricia A. Straat, were then left to pick up the pieces as best they could.

Levin and Straat began to search for a simulated Martian soil, one containing hydrogen peroxide for instance, that would reproduce by nonbiological means the same effects which had been obtained on Mars. In almost ten years of searching they found none. Meanwhile, the GC/MS experiment was belatedly tested against Antarctic soils, and it failed to detect organic material of biological origin which was known with certainty to be there. From these belated tests it became evident that the GC/MS had only a poor sensitivity. Unless the number of microorganisms in a gram of soil exceeded 100 million, the GC/MS experiment could not find them, whereas the LR experiment was estimated from laboratory calibration to be capable of detecting the much lower concentration of 10 thousand microorganisms to a gram of Martian soil; in other words, the LR experiment was apparently many thousands of times more sensitive than the GC/MS experiment. After these facts emerged, Levin and Straat attempted to correct the original erroneous announcement by NASA. Giving full documentation, they have said that the Viking experiments really did find life on Mars, agreeing with an earlier positive statement to this effect by Robert Jastrow.

Was this a highly expensive muddle, or was it a deliberate mistake? We have encountered so much emotional opposition to the concept of life existing outside the Earth, especially in the United States by opponents of creationism, that we have to suspect the latter, although we acknowledge that muddle is more common in the world than deception. At all events, we suspect that those responsible for the original announcement by NASA were not unhappy with it.

The gases of the atmospheres of the planets have myriads of small particles similar in size to bacteria suspended in them. The particles produce cloud and haze effects from which some of their properties can be inferred, particularly their refractive indices. A few years ago we drew up a table, reproduced here as Table 9.1, comparing several astronomical and biological refractive indices.

Table 9.1 ASTRONOMICAL AND BIOLOGICAL REFRACTIVE INDICES.

Location of astronomical particles	Refractive index of astronomical particles	Biological particles	Refractive index of biological particles
Interstellar space	1.16	Bacteria (dry)	1.17
Atmosphere of Venus	1.44 ± 0.02	Bacterial spores (wet)	1.44
Atmosphere of Jupiter	1.38	Bacteria (wet)	1.39

For sources see: F. Hoyle and N. C. Wickramasinghe, MEMOIRS OF THE INSTITUTE OF FUNDAMENTAL STUDIES, *Sri Lanka, 1982, No. 1.*

Small particles in the Solar System are seen most spectacularly in the rings of Saturn. Astronomers were astonished when the Voyager missions revealed the immense multiplicity of rings – a few had been expected, but nothing like the many hundreds of small ringlets that were actually found. Embedded in the ringlets were small satellites, hitherto unknown, which became referred to as 'shepherd satellites' because the intricate ringlet structure seemed to be due to a subtle gravitational control exercised by these small bodies. The idea is that an initially uniform disc of small particles revolving around Saturn would break up into many ringlets as the small bodies were captured by the planet's gravity. While there is almost surely some truth in this idea, we suspect there to be considerably more to the matter. The shepherd satellites are extraordinarily like the nuclei of comets, from which the small particles could have been expelled from the satellites in the manner of the recently observed outbursts from Comet Halley. However, Saturn could not capture passing comets in any simple way. Only the break up of a passing larger body with a retention of some pieces seems possible, with the retained pieces becoming the shepherd satellites. Similar considerations apply to the rings around Jupiter, Uranus and Neptune which have been discovered only in recent years.

One of us recalls a story told by mountaineers in the Rockies, of how they returned to camp one day to find a bear lying dead beside a nearby stream. The manner in which the bear had died was remarkable. It had exploded, with a great open chasm around its waist. What had happened was that the bear, raiding the camp in search of food, had come on a large bag of dehydrated apple rings which it had consumed with relish. Feeling thirsty, it had gone to the stream to drink, and the almost instant expansion that occurred as the water mixed with the dried apple had created a surge of pressure which had done the rest. This is an example of the inability of even strong material like rock to cope with irresistible internal pressures that are generated when chemical reactions take place inside them, especially reactions leading to an efflux of gas. The whole rock is cracked open like the bear – the origin, we suspect, of the cracks which cross the satellite Europa in the system of Jupiter.

Bacteria can survive great pressures as well as exceedingly low pressures. Dr Al-Mufti applied a pressure of about 10 tonnes per square centimetre to bacteria mixed with potassium bromide simply, using a standard press used for the preparation of the discs used in infrared spectroscopy. He then dissolved away the potassium bromide and found he could successfully culture the bacteria, thereby proving that bacteria could survive the pressures deep inside the Moon and other satellites of the Solar System. Thus the interiors of bodies as well as their surfaces and atmospheres are possible habitats for microorganisms. A direct and dramatic confirmation of this has come from the recent recovery of colonies of bacteria from deep drills into the Earth's crust reaching depths of 7 kilometres or more.

There is an immense class of bacteria, known as chemo-autotrophes. They depend for their existence on chemical reactions of very diverse kinds, but have the common property of yielding a little energy and being far too sluggish under purely inorganic conditions. These bacteria are the devices by which matter reaches its lowest energy state at typical planetary temperatures. Where we see that the lowest energy state has been achieved in situations that would otherwise be too sluggish, it is a fair inference that bacteria have been at work. To give an important example, an inorganic mixture of hydrogen and carbon dioxide could be stored at room temperature essentially for ever, yet it would never go by chemical reactions to methane. A carefully made hot-water catalyst could convert such a mixture to methane and other hydrocarbons, but such exceedingly delicate catalysts would almost instantly be destroyed in the presence of gases containing sulphur compounds, such as exist under astronomical conditions. Even under carefully controlled industrial conditions, delicate metal catalysts cannot compete economically in the production of hydrocarbons with oil at $20 per barrel. Yet biological catalysts are able to convert hydrogen and carbon dioxide or carbon monoxide to methane with ease. There is indeed a class of simple bacteria with just this property, known as the methanogens. Now, methane is found in quantity in the atmospheres of the four large outer planets – Jupiter, Saturn, Uranus and Neptune – where its presence is indicative of bacterial action on a huge scale. One can go still further and say that, if alternative purely inorganic means were possible for taking matter to its lowest energy state at planetary temperatures, the whole chemo-autotrophic class of bacteria, including the methanogens, would be bypassed and could not exist.

We would not urge that any single topic considered in this chapter be regarded as more than an indication of the presence of microorganisms outside the Earth. Taken together, however, all pointing in the same direction, they do add up to what can be considered a fair test of the theory. Even so, the ability to test the theory by reference to distant bodies in the Solar System, bodies which can at best be visited only briefly and very incompletely, must be regarded as secondary to tests made here on the Earth. With the Earth receiving 10^{21} bacteria each year, and perhaps ten thousand times as many viral particles as well, the possibilities for testing the theory close to home are immense.

It may seem obvious to the reader that a direct test of the theory could be made by sampling the Earth's upper atmosphere for incoming microorganisms. However, in advance of such a test being made it should be agreed as to what is to be accepted as a positive result for the theory. If, when viable microorganisms are found at great heights in the stratosphere and mesosphere, critics then maintain that the microorganisms have been carried upwards from ground-level, no positive result is possible, and one has to accept the position that the theory can only be falsified but not proved in this way, a somewhat less than satisfactory position. We saw in Chapter 8 that the stratosphere is a region where vertical movements of air are extremely feeble, so that diffusion upwards against gravity acting on particles the sizes of bacteria would not be expected to take place beyond the base of the stratosphere. But with critics free to say anything they please, the best one can claim is not proof, but a further consistency check on the theory.

Balloon flights into the stratosphere, up to heights of about 40 kilometres, made in the early 1960s obtained viable microorganisms that could be cultured by relatively simple means. The equipment was sterilized before each flight, and two similar experimental packages were flown, one package being exposed to the atmosphere and the other not, the unexposed package serving as a control. Since viable microorganisms were not obtained in the control package, those obtained in the exposed package would appear to have been genuinely atmospheric.

The results showed that there were 0.01–0.1 viable bacteria per cubic metre. It seemed puzzling that the higher value of 0.1 per cubic metre was obtained for the high stratosphere and 0.01 per cubic metre for the lower stratosphere, just the opposite of what would be expected if the bacteria were diffusing upwards from ground-level. NASA, which had provided the funds for the balloon flights and experiments, dealt with the puzzle by simply withdrawing funds for any further flights. There is actually a simple explanation of why, with the bacteria incident from outside the Earth, a low value for the density of those which remain viable is to be expected near the base of the stratosphere. It is that sulphurous gases given out by volcanoes tend to be concentrated there, and many of the bacteria are probably killed or rendered inactive by becoming coated with sulphuric acid.

Taking a viable bacterial density of 0.1 per cubic metre as representative of the whole stratosphere, it is easily calculated that the total number of bacteria resident in the stratosphere at any moment should be about 10^{18}, and since bacteria fall to ground-level from the stratosphere in about a year, the annual incidence at ground-level of viable bacteria culturable by rather simple means should be 10^{18}. If this number is increased to allow for those bacteria requiring other means of culturing, as for instance methanogens requiring hydrogen and carbon dioxide as nutrients, and also increased to allow for those bacteria that have been killed or become inactive, the result becomes consistent with the larger number obtained in Chapter 8.

We saw in Chapter 8 that in the mesosphere, above the strato-sphere, bacteria fall rapidly under gravity, so that their density in the mesosphere is expected to be several orders of magnitude less than in the stratosphere. Yet in the late 1970s viable bacteria were collected from the mesosphere. Rockets rather than balloons have to be used in the mesosphere. A rocket was flown to an altitude of about 80 kilometres, where it disgorged two sterilized instrument packages which then descended on parachutes. As in the balloon flights, one package was opened to the atmosphere and the other not, the unopened package serving as a control. In two short series of flights about thirty cultures were obtained from packages opened to the atmosphere at heights between 50 and 80 kilometres, and none was obtained from the unopened control packages. The cultured bacteria were said to be all heavily pigmented, with the implication that the pigmentation served as protection against solar ultraviolet radiation. The latter experiments were carried out by Soviet scientists. As soon as we expressed interest, particularly with respect to the possibility that the bacteria might have come from outside the Earth, their reaction was exactly the same as the reaction of NASA had been: to drop the whole thing like a hot brick.

A final consistency check! We understand from experts in the field of cloud seeding and rain formation that bacteria are far more effective as condensation nuclei than any form of inorganic particle – far more effective than silver iodide, for example. The concentration of so-called ice nuclei high in the troposphere and lower stratosphere is usually given as about 100 per cubic metre. If each such nucleus is formed around a bacterium, the total for the whole atmosphere, of volume 10^{19} cubic metres, would be about 10^{21}, and this would also be the order of the annual incidence at ground-level, closely consistent with the estimate in Chapter 8. It is interesting that this is also the order of the number of raindrops that fall to the ground over the whole Earth in the course of a year.

CHAPTER TEN

The pathogenic test

When a bacterium replicates (one makes two, two make four, and so on) the sudden and rapid growth in its progeny is similar to what happens inside a Geiger counter to make it click. When a viral particle attacks some host or other, its growth into many similar viral particles is also similar in nature to the 'tripping' of a Geiger counter. In all three cases there is an initial single trigger, hard to observe by itself, yielding a burst of products which taken together are readily observable. Now, according to the theory set out in the previous chapters, an immense number of bacteria and viruses of all kinds fall each year from space onto the terrestrial ensemble of plants and animals, which we can think of as providing a nutrient medium for the incoming microorganisms. If some interact strongly to produce cultures, this will be a situation potentially like the detection of high-speed particles, in effect using the terrestrial plants and animals as detectors which produce outbursts of replication that should be far more readily observable than the original microorganisms themselves. This provides a far more straightforward and much less expensive method of testing the theory than the use of balloons, rockets and satellites.

The idea that particular human diseases are spread by contagion, being passed from one person to another, is to be found from the beginnings of medical history, because from straightforward observations those who attended the sick could see that for some diseases the facts could not be explained otherwise. Thus of the plague that devastated the ancient city of Athens in 430 BC, Thucydides wrote:

For a while physicians sought to apply remedies in ignorance, but it was in vain, and they themselves were most prone to perish because they came into most frequent contact with it. No other human art was of any avail, and as to supplications in temples, inquiries of oracles, and the like, they were all useless; and at last men were overpowered by the calamity and gave them all up.

It was much the same during the infamous Black Death of AD 1348–50, people praying in the churches and it proving useless – indeed, the death rate was highest in religious institutions, where the fleas (which actually carried the disease) circulated among the monks at maximum rates. Those who lived through the trauma of the Black Death must have been much puzzled by what they saw. The contagion idea suggested that those whose unhappy job it was to collect the bodies of the dead would be particularly at risk, and doubtless this led to the payment rate for the job going high enough for some to volunteer for it. Yet the risk did not prove high, for surprisingly, as it seemed, there was no unusual mortality among the body collectors. The reason was that the disease-carrying fleas quitted their human hosts immediately after death. Statistics show that the body-collectors, mostly out in the open air, did far better than the monks praying together for much of the time.

Nevertheless, there was a widespread view that the Black Death – bubonic plague caused by a bacterium – came from outside, from the skies. This alternative view of the source of some diseases is also a theme occurring throughout medical history, and if one accepts the reported evidence one can see why. Of the Black Death itself, Pedro Carbonell recorded that the disease first broke out in Aragon (where he was the Court Archivist), in the city of Teruel. Since Teruel is an inland city, this posed the problem of how the disease had spread there from its earlier appearance in Italy. By ship was not the answer;

by air appeared to be. The ultimate source of the Plague of Athens evidently puzzled Thucydides: 'It is said to have previously smitten many places, particularly Lemnos; but there is no record of so great a pestilence occurring elsewhere, or of so great a destruction of human life.' The same problem of the ultimate source of those diseases which spread by contagion has confronted commentators over the ages, and nobody, even in modern times, has offered a convincing earthbound answer to it.

Bubonic plague is not primarily a human disease. The bacterium *Pasteurella pestis* attacks many species of rodent, its first target. Because the black rat happened to live in close proximity to humans, nesting in the walls of houses, the physical separation of people from the black rat was small and could be bridged by fleas, which carried the bacterium from the blood of rats to the blood of humans. This transfer process was not welcomed by the fleas, who preferred to stay with the rats, quitting them only as their hosts died from the disease. Although human–flea–human transfer of the bacterium presumably occurred, it does not seem to have been sufficient to maintain the disease, which died out as the supply of rats became exhausted.

Bubonic plague has appeared in sudden bursts separated by many centuries, and it is difficult to understand where *P. pestis* went into hiding during the long intermissions. A somewhat ambiguous reference occurs in the Old Testament, at a date of about 1200 BC, when the Philistines are said to have been attacked by 'emrods [buboes] in their secret parts . . .' as a reprisal from God for an attack on the Hebrews. A clear reference to plague occurs in an Indian medical treatise written in the fifth century BC, in which people are advised to leave houses and other buildings 'when rats fall from the roofs above, jump about and die'.

There may have been an outbreak of plague during the first century AD, with centres of the disease in Syria and North Africa, but between the first and sixth centuries there were no known occurrences. In AD 540, a pandemic covering the Near East, North Africa and southern Europe may have had a death toll that reached 100 million, with more than 5000 dying each day in Constantinople alone. This was the so-called Plague of Justinian, the Roman Emperor at the time.

Bubonic plague then seems to have disappeared from our planet for eight centuries, until it reappeared with shattering personal and social consequences in the Black Death of 1348–50. Thereafter, the disease smouldered with minor outbreaks until the mid-seventeenth century; for two centuries it seemed once again to have died out, only for it to reappear in China in 1894. In India, it killed some thirteen million people in the years up to the First World War.

By working from historical records of the first outbreaks of plague in various population centres, Dr E. Carpentier drew up the contours shown in Figure 10.1 marking the spread of the Black Death across Europe. The contour for 31 December 1347, though, appears to have been drawn to fit a belief rather than from documentary facts. The belief is that the disease was brought into Europe via the Tartars, who had besieged the Genoese base of Caffa in the Crimea; the line of December 1347 is said to mark the voyage of Genoese ships back to Italy. There are doubts about this, however, since the much better-attested contour for December 1348 seems to be headed to intersect the one for December 1347 somewhere in the region of the Danube delta, which from the nature of the contours – the first outbreaks at the various locations – is an impossible condition.

The contours in Figure 10.1 have been interpreted by orthodox opinion as steps in the march of an army of plague-infested rats. Humans with the disease collapsed on the spot; we think afflicted rats must surely have done the same. To argue that stricken rats set out on a journey that took them in six months, not merely from southern to northern France, but even across the Alpine massif, borders on the ridiculous.

It apparently stretches credulity too far to argue that the advancing army of stricken rats also managed to swim the English Channel, and it is usually said that the Black Death reached England by ship. Yet the contours in Figure 10.1 are of quite the wrong shape for boats to have played a significant role in spreading the disease. If *P. pestis* had been carried by sea, the earliest contour would be wrapped around the coastline from the Mediterranean to northern Europe, with subsequent contours then filling in gradually towards central Europe. Not only this, but if the bacillus had travelled by sea, the coast of Portugal would have been seriously affected, whereas the

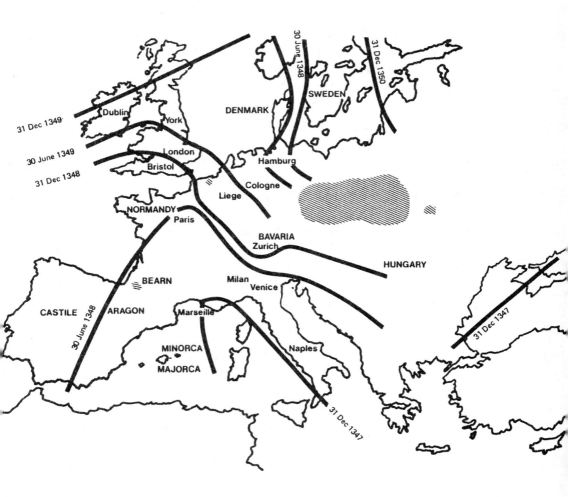

Figure 10.1 The spread of the Black Death in Europe (after Dr E. Carpentier). The contour lines indicate the broad spread of the plague, and the hatched areas show where the plague had little or no effect.

evidence is that the plague scarcely penetrated to Castile, Galicia or Portugal.

There are many descriptions of communities that isolated themselves deliberately from the outside world, many such descriptions from English villages. Yet isolation was to no avail. The Black Death would strike suddenly, and within a week the people in such a community would be just as affected by the disease as everyone else.

What remarkable rats they were. To have crossed the sea and to have reached into remote English villages, and yet to have effectively bypassed the cities of Milan, Liège and Nuremberg! To have reached into remote villages and yet to have largely spared the areas shaded in Figure 10.1, especially the extended area in Bohemia and southern Poland. The astonishing reason offered for this behaviour is indicative of the state of mind engendered by orthodox theory. The rats, it is said, disliked the food available to them in these regions.

We have remarked above that as early as the fifth century BC Indian doctors had noted the connection of plague with rats. Yet medieval doctors had no such thoughts. It was their overwhelming view that the pestilence had its origin in the air – 'poisoned' air was the widely favoured explanation. It has been fashionable to decry this view as an unsubstantiated superstition, although the state of technical understanding in fourteenth-century Europe was higher than it had been at any earlier stage of human history. Indeed, unless one is prejudiced by modern superstitions, the contours in Figure 10.1 are a clear indication that *P. pestis* hit Europe from the air. There was no marching army of plague-stricken rats. The rats died in the places where they were infected, just as humans did. By falling from the air, *P. pestis* had no difficulty at all in crossing the Alps, or in crossing the English Channel. Remote English villages were hit, however determinedly they sought to seal themselves off from the outside world, because the plague bacillus descended upon them from above; and against an aerial assault all the precautions taken were of no consequence. Milan, Liège and Nuremberg went comparatively unscathed because it is in the nature of incidence from the upper atmosphere that there will be odd spots where a pathogen does not fall. So too did Bohemia and southern Poland escape, even though these areas grow food just as palatable to rats as food everywhere else.

There are three stages in the development of knowledge: the first stage is characterized by humility, the second by prejudice and the third by certainty. In the first stage people accept that they do not know the answer to certain problems. They content themselves with the relatively simple task of describing what happens as accurately as possible, so that from a historical point of view what is said in the first stage is usually reliable. In the second stage, however, the situation becomes garbled, because people knowing a little but not sufficient distort what they report in order to fit their preconceptions. In the third stage, knowledge has become essentially complete, as it has in some parts of physics, and all emotion and even interest has gone out of the situation, leaving certain knowledge simply as a tool to be used, not to be argued about.

As far as the causes of diseases are concerned, the people of medieval times lived in the first of these three stages, whereas we in modern times live in the second, the stage where facts are often distorted or ignored. We saw in Chapter 6 that the writer in the issue of *Nature* for 3 February 1870 of an article entitled 'The atmospheric-germ theory' was quite prepared to ignore the facts of bacteriology in order to go along with the prejudice that 'germs' did not come through the atmosphere. The date of this article corresponds in medical history to the transition between the first of the above stages and the second, a transition largely caused by public awareness of 'Darwin's geocentric theory' and by a rapidly growing need to make respect for the facts subservient to belief in that theory.

Half a century earlier, doctors had still been content to base their beliefs on what they actually observed for themselves. In 1813, Robert Thomas had written in his book *The Modern Practice of Physic*: 'By some physicians influenza was supposed to be contagious; by others not so; indeed, its wide and rapid spread made many suspect some more generally prevailing cause in the atmosphere.' If physicians had thus continued to study influenza with their eyes, correct answers would surely have been arrived at before the close of the nineteenth century, answers such as we shall report in the next chapter. Instead, the intellectual miasma spread by 'Darwin's theory' increasingly closed the minds of successive generations of students. By the early twentieth century a society departing almost indefinitely from the truth had been produced by the process we discussed in our opening chapter, a society that could ignore clear-cut disproofs of contagion as the cause of the rapid spread of influenza, as in this quotation: 'You have the short days, the hard cold weather, and you only make

20 to 30 miles a day over unbroken trails. The conditions there are such as have never happened before in the history of the Territory.' This was Governor Riggs of Alaska, speaking at a meeting of the Senate Committee of Appropriations held on 16 January 1919. The governor was referring to the spread of influenza in the late months of 1918 throughout the huge territory of Alaska, in such physical conditions that it was essentially impossible for people to travel except over very small distances.

Reference to extreme cold makes it likely that there had been an overturn in the atmosphere, bringing exceedingly cold air from great heights down to ground-level. Of the same deadly worldwide influenza pandemic of 1918, Louis Weinstein wrote in the issue of the *New England Journal of Medicine* for May 1976:

The influenza pandemic of 1918 occurred in three waves. The first appeared in the winter and spring of 1917–18.... This wave was characterised by high attack rates (50 per cent of the world's population were affected) but by very low fatality rates. The lethal second wave, which started at Fort Devens in Ayer, Massachusetts on September 12, 1918, involved almost the entire world over a very short time. Its epidemiologic behaviour was most unusual. Although person-to-person spread occurred in local areas, the disease appeared on the same day in widely separated parts of the world on the one hand, but, on the other, took days to weeks to spread relatively short distances. It was detected in Boston and Bombay on the same day, but took three weeks before it reached New York city, despite the fact that there was considerable travel between the two cities.

How, in 1918, when the journey between Boston and Bombay took many weeks by sea, could essentially the first appearances of the second wave have been in these two cities? And why if the influenza virus could apparently travel at lightning speed did it take three weeks to get from Boston to New York? Another example is found in a report of an influenza epidemic of the late 1940s on the island of Sardinia:

We were able to verify ... the appearance of influenza in shepherds who were living for a long time alone, in solitary open country far from any inhabited centre; this occurred absolutely contemporaneously with the appearance of influenza in the nearest inhabited centres. (F. Magrassi, *Minerva Medica Torino*, 1949, **40**, 565).

For a disease to spread by contagion to epidemic proportions, the basic mathematical condition of a nuclear explosion must be satisfied: the fission of each nucleus must induce the fission of more than one other nucleus, the necessary condition for a chain reaction to grow. That is to say, each victim of a contagiously spreading disease must on average pass the causative agent of the disease to more than one other subsequent victim. For diseases like influenza with short incubation periods (about three days), the difference between the margin of criticality and an exceedingly rapid spread is rather small. If, on average, each victim infects only 0.95 subsequent victims, the epidemic will not run, whereas for twice this value, with each victim infecting 1.9 others on average, a worldwide pandemic could occur in only three months. Yet a difference of only a factor of two here is very small compared with factors of more than a hundred which exist in the population density between heavily populated towns and remote country areas, which should make far more difference than a factor of two in the transmissibility factor between victim and victim. Thus one would expect epidemics propagated by contagion to spread through a heavily populated area to its less populated margin as a city population faded into a country population, where eventually the epidemic would fail to run. This did happen for epidemics of truly contagious diseases such as smallpox, but it is not what happens for many diseases, particularly respiratory diseases such as influenza, where town and country are affected essentially equally both in time and severity, as the above quotation from F. Magrassi shows to have been the case in the epidemic outbreak on the island of Sardinia, an island which in 1948 had little in the way of rapid communication between one part and another.

The information necessary to settle the issue of atmospheric incidence versus contagion lies readily to hand, in a comparison of the chances of people living in remote country areas, compared with those of people living in heavily populated cities, of contracting various diseases. Dr Pat Jenkins, Community Health Officer for the City of Cardiff, preserved data obtained separately from the heavily populated Cardiff city area in South Wales and from the Vale of Glamorgan, much of which is very rural. The occurrence of cases on a quarterly (three-monthly) basis was available for three diseases: measles (virus), infective jaundice (virus) and whooping cough

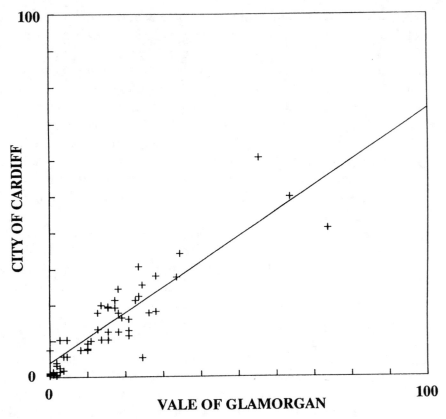

Figure 10.2a Quarterly incidence of whooping cough, measles and infective jaundice in the City of Cardiff and the Vale of Glamorgan, for quarters where the incidence was comparatively light, in the years 1979–83. The numbers have been adjusted to a standard population of 100,000.

(bacillus). Because the numbers varied between quarters of light occurrence and quarters of severe occurrence, we found it useful for display purposes to separate the two, plotting first the light quarters only to obtain the correlation diagram shown in Figure 10.2a, in which numbers of cases have been adjusted to a standard of 100,000 people. Within the statistical scatter there was no difference between town and country, a result which evidently supports a general atmospheric origin for the three diseases, not contagion.

Figure 10.2b, drawn similarly to Figure 10.2a except for a change of scale, includes quarters of the year when the numbers of cases were

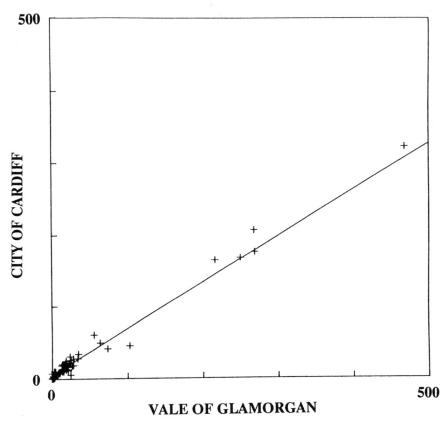

Figure 10.2*b*   Quarterly incidence of whooping cough, measles and infective jaundice in the City of Cardiff and the Vale of Glamorgan, including quarters in which the incidence was comparatively heavy, in the years 1979–83. The numbers have been adjusted to a standard population of 100,000.

exceptionally large in the data supplied to us by Dr Jenkins. We found it impressive that a correlation line of the same slope as before fits the quarters of high numbers just as well as it did for the less severe quarters. There is evidently no indication of the greater risk to city populations required by the contagion theory. The situation is as it should be if the pathogens responsible for the diseases in question (measles, infective jaundice, whooping cough) fell from the atmosphere more or less equally on town and country with, if anything, a slight bias towards the more open spaces of the countryside, the opposite of what one would expect for the contagion theory.

CHAPTER ELEVEN

The decisive tests

An immense amount of information is constantly being thrown away as bacteria and viruses from space interact with terrestrial plants and animals. Only if we ourselves are affected, either in our own health or economically through blighted crops or in the diseases of domesticated animals, do we pay much attention to what is going on, and even then most of the information is unfortunately lost. Nevertheless, the situation remains perpetually informative. This is because new important data are coming along all the time. Even though almost everything that happens in 1993 is being wasted, a further avalanche of data will become available in 1994, and again in 1995. . . . So what is happening cannot really be lost.

We have found it surprising how much can be discovered for the cost of only a few postage stamps, something we learned from the example of the Dutch physician J. J. van Loghem from as long ago as 1926. In his book *The Common Cold* (Weidenfeld & Nicolson, London, 1965), Sir Christopher Andrewes recounts the story:

Van Loghem in 1925–26 carried out a postal canvas of about seven thousand persons in different parts of the Netherlands over a period from September to June. He was concerned to find out about the occurrence of colds in relation to time and space. He analysed the results of his canvas and plotted them as curves. The curves showing the incidence of colds week by week were quite complicated ones. The astonishing thing was that the complicated curves from one part of Holland could be fitted over those from another part of the country and the fit was remarkably close. This showed two things: first the time of rise and fall of colds was almost the same in different places, and second, the extent of the rise was the same. Van Loghem argued, not unreasonably, that all this just would not fit in with the idea of a stepwise person-to-person spread. Such findings are not isolated; very similar things have been reported by workers in the United States.

The only reasonable doubt one could have about van Loghem's report was whether he had plotted his curves correctly, but once similar results had been obtained by others, this doubt was removed and the picture became clear. Since the world does not contain self-contradictions, the situation for the common cold was settled. The common cold had a cause which affected a whole nation essentially simultaneously, and not all the king's men would ever change the fact. It did not need anything else to show that, so far as the common cold was concerned, the contagion theory was dead, as long ago as 1926.

It is the common experience of general practitioners in northern temperate latitudes that their surgeries normally fill to overflowing in February and March, at the time of year when there is a dramatic descent through the stratosphere by small particles; evidence of this descent has been shown in Figure 8.1 of Chapter 8. Figure 11.1 shows in detail the clockwork-like regularity of one of the regular crop of late-winter diseases with which we are thus afflicted.

Accepting that the cause of the regularity of Figure 11.1 is a stratospheric vertical movement bringing the causative virus down to ground-level, it necessarily follows that a similar effect must occur in the southern hemisphere of the Earth with winter and summer interchanged, the bad months of January to March in the north becoming July to September in the south. We do not have reliable southern data for respiratory syncytial disease, but some data for influenza exist, influenza also being a member of the usual winter crop of diseases experienced in the north. The expected alternation

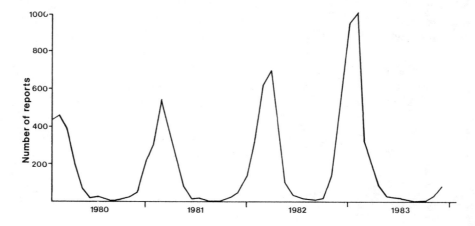

Figure 11.1 The incidence of respiratory syncytial infections in England and Wales (*Communicable Disease Report 83/49*, Communicable Disease Surveillance Centre, London, 1983).

between summer and winter is well shown in Figure 11.2, with no significant alternation occurring in the tropics.

We have chosen to show the data for Sweden rather than Britain, not because there is any important difference between Sweden and Britain, but to bring out the point that the simple physical cold of winter is not a relevant factor. Sweden has a really cold winter, whereas Australia has a mild winter, not much cooler than a Swedish summer. If simple exposure to cold were important, the effect would long ago have been demonstrated under controlled conditions in the laboratory, which it has not been.

It was pointed out in Chapter 8 that, to the extent to which the surface of the Earth may be considered smooth, bacteria and viruses falling from the atmosphere can be expected to reach ground-level at much the same time along a particular parallel of latitude. With the exception of the Rocky Mountains of North America, there is a belt around the Earth from about 45 to 60°N where the land is not much above sea-level, and where for places near a particular parallel of latitude the rules of simultaneity should apply. Edgar Hope-Simpson has noted the remarkable similarity shown in Figure 11.3

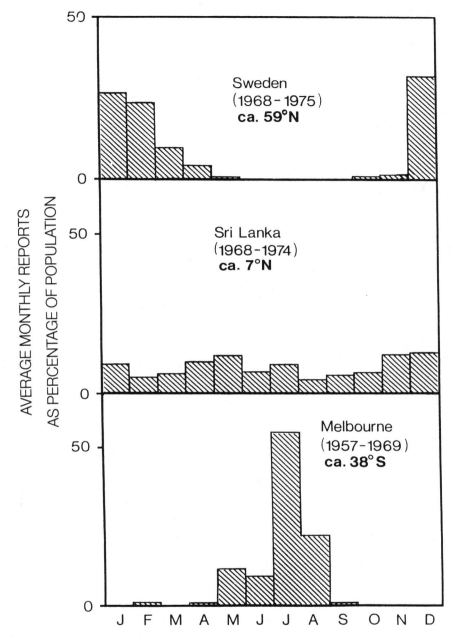

Figure 11.2 Incidence of influenza A in three separate countries.

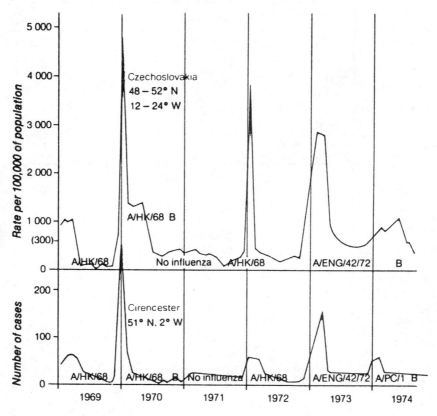

Figure 11.3 The attack rates of influenza in Prague and Cirencester (after E. Hope-Simpson).

between his influenza records for the Cirencester district of England and the Prague district of Czechoslovakia.

Hope-Simpson has played an outstanding role in modern times in questioning the validity of the contagion theory, both for influenza and for the common cold. As a general practitioner, he had the opportunity to test the contagion theory in a decisive way. In the two heavy influenza years of 1968/9 and 1969/70, he observed an adequately large number of households in which at least one case of influenza occurred. He then noted other cases in the households following the initial case, arguing that members of households –

112

particularly husbands and wives – are in such close contact that contagion, if it occurs at all significantly, should surely operate to produce an abnormal incidence of cases in a typical incubation period of about 3 days after the first case. But, as Figure 11.4 shows, this was emphatically not what happened. There was no peak of cases two or three days after the first, subsequent cases were more or less uniformly distributed over many days, and in total they did not

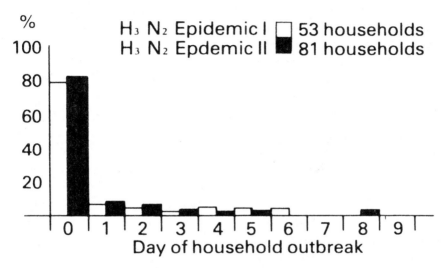

Figure 11.4 Percentage attack rates in households where one member succumbed to influenza in the epidemics of 1968/9 and 1969/70 at Cirencester, England, according to data from E. Hope-Simpson.

exceed what was to be expected for the population at large. Just as van Loghem's results were reproduced by other workers, so Hope-Simpson's results were verified in 1981 by a team of British public-health officials.

We remarked in Chapter 8 that viruses fall from the stratosphere to ground-level inside either raindrops or ice crystals (snowflakes). To become free to circulate in the air immediately above ground-level, it is necessary for raindrops to evaporate just before reaching the ground. This leads to irregularities in the distribution of viruses, both from place to place and also over the course of time. Because snow falls only when the lower air is cold, it follows that during snowy weather, such as occurred in Britain in January and February 1985, there can be little in the way of a release of viruses into the lower atmosphere. Evaporation is too limited for snowflakes containing viruses to satisfy the condition of evaporating away just before they reach ground-level. This is why cold, brisk winter weather is traditionally regarded as healthy, and why warmer, damp, clammy and especially foggy or misty winter weather is regarded as unhealthy, again demonstrating that the physical cold of winter is not a relevant factor. The picture also explains why places at ground-level where surface winds tend to blow frequently, thus quickly removing any patches of virus that happen to be released at those places, are regarded as healthy places, as for instance seaside resorts and other favoured retirement places.

Few cases of influenza were reported anywhere in the world up to mid-February during the winter of 1984/5, an unusual situation that permitted our colleague Dr John Watkins to analyse acute upper-respiratory-tract diseases other than influenza with respect to house-holds, in the same way as Hope-Simpson had done for influenza. His results, for a total of 80 households, are shown in Figure 11.5. They too demonstrate a lack of contagion, but now for acute upper-respiratory ailments in general.

Dr Watkins also found another way to demonstrate the general unimportance of contagion in the spread of upper-respiratory ail-ments. From the records at his practice, he identified 16 pairs of twins with ages between six months and fourteen years. Of the 118 instances in which one twin was consulted for acute upper-respiratory infection, the corresponding twin succumbed to a similar infection in only 28 instances, which was not much different from what one would expect to find in the population at large. Despite the fact that twins in this age range spend almost all their time together, giving contagion a maximum opportunity, there was little evidence of it. Even if the 28 instances out of 118 were all attributed to contagion, the probability of contagion causing twin-to-twin infections would be only $28/118 = 0.24$, far too low a transmissibility factor for any epidemic to run.

In view of all this clear-cut evidence against the person-to-person

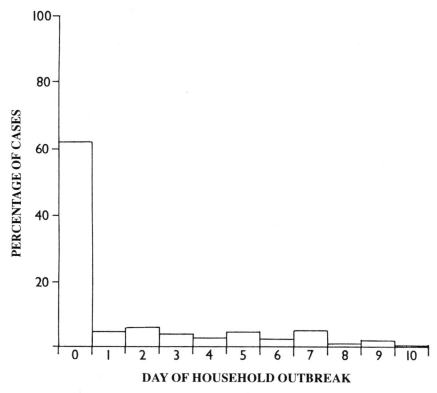

Figure 11.5 Percentage incidence of acute upper-respiratory-tract infections in households where one member succumbs to illness on day 0, from data collected by Dr John Watkins in 1984/5.

transmission of respiratory viral diseases, the reader may well wonder how contagion ever achieved any standing as a theory. Part of the answer is that some diseases, the dreaded smallpox for example, really do seem to be contagious. The other part is the influence of dubious 'facts' which have become widely believed because the education system leads us to accept what our teachers tell us. When we first approached this whole subject in the late 1970s, we read in textbooks that the person-to-person transmission of influenza had been proved from the very high attack rates of the disease which occurred in institutions such as military barracks and boarding schools. Not being students with an imperative need to pass examinations, we were determined to check this statement, and in the winter of 1977/8 an opportunity for doing so presented itself. That winter there was a peculiar return of an influenza subtype (H_1N_1) which had not been experienced since the 1950s, and against which no child of school age had any established immunity. Following van Loghem, we made a postal canvas of a large number of boarding schools involving a total of more than 20,000 pupils. Of these, the number of influenza victims was estimated to be 8880, with an average attack rate of about 30 per cent. All the diagnoses had been made by school medical staffs in advance of our enquiries, and so the data we received were in no way correlated with our investigation itself (correlations between data and enquiries being the besetting sin of many epidemiological investigations).

Figure 11.6 shows numbers of schools plotted against attack rates. Only three schools out of more than a hundred at the extreme upper end of a steeply falling distribution had the very high attack rates which had been claimed to be the norm. So why had such a claim ever been made? The article described in Chapter 6, 'The atmospheric-germ theory', which appeared in the issue of *Nature* for Thursday, 3 February 1870, showed a mentality that would say anything it could get away with, even to the extent of denying the facts of bacteriology by casting doubt on the validity of the work by Louis Pasteur. This was an example of a phenomenon that has grown with the years, to the point where, today, it is endemic throughout science. There is essentially no limit to what will be said in support of dogma, provided those who say it think they will not be challenged. One of the hardest aspects of working at the frontiers of science is to know what is germane and what is deceitful. It often happens that, if much time, effort and money would have to be expended in calling someone's bluff, one is essentially forced to make decisions about what is true and what is false on personality judgements.

More emerged from our postal canvas than we can describe here, but a few of the other results may be briefly mentioned. Figure 11.7 compares attack rates experienced by boarders and day pupils for those schools in our canvas which took both. Each plotted point in the diagram represents a particular school, and the attack rates for

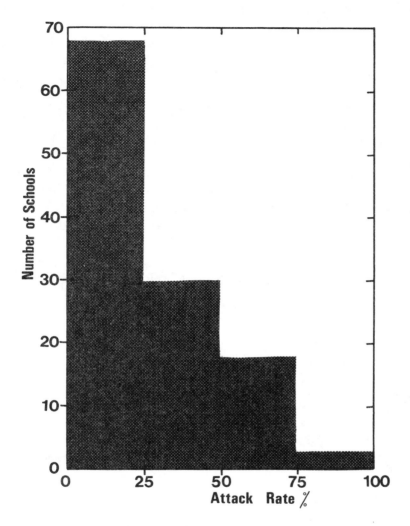

Figure 11.6 Histogram showing the distribution of influenza among independent schools in England and Wales during the 1977/8 pandemic.

day pupils and boarders can be read off on the vertical and horizontal axes, respectively. Despite the claim that boarders suffer heavily through sleeping communally in dormitories, there was little evidence of it. Whatever slight bias there is in Figure 11.7 about a 45° line disappears for a line of slope 40°, which is within the expected

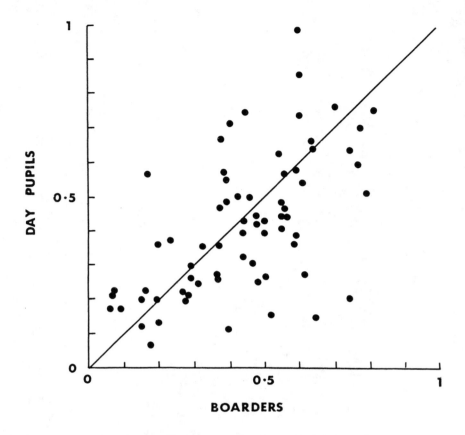

Figure 11.7 Correlation of attack rates for day pupils and boarders, for schools which had a mixture of both, during the 1977/8 influenza pandemic in England and Wales.

statistical fluctuation. There are many instances in which the day pupils experienced considerably higher attack rates than boarders. This is difficult to explain in terms of person-to-person transmission, for we would have to suppose that, after leaving school, the day pupils encountered more seriously infective contacts than were present at school, and that they did so systematically, in order to create the high attack rates of above 70 per cent found for the day pupils in some of the schools.

Attack rates of around 30 per cent proved the most useful for studying variations within school boundaries, since very high attack rates evidently preclude variations being found, while low attack rates gave inadequate statistical weight. Eton College had 441 victims among 1248 pupils for an attack rate of 35 per cent, with high statistical weight because of the large number of pupils. We were fortunate that Dr J. Bristoe, the Medical Officer at Eton, had for a long time been trying to puzzle out how to explain his observations in terms of pupil-to-pupil transmission. He had collected comprehensive information on the distribution of victims in some 25 school houses. The houses averaged about 50 pupils each, so 17 would be the mean number of victims if cases were distributed randomly. Such numbers were very suitable for computing standard deviations (a statistical measure of departure from randomness); the

Figure 11.8 Standard deviations (sig) of attack rates of influenza from the mean attack rate for the 25 school houses at Eton College during the 1978/9 pandemic. The deviations are relative to the standard deviation computed house by house.

results are shown in Figure 11.8. Two houses had excess morbidities of 4 standard deviations, two had deficits of about 4 standard deviations, and one showed the remarkable deficit of 6 standard deviations. Since pupils in the different houses mixed together in classes and at games, these enormous fluctuations from a random distribution are quite inexplicable, it seems to us, in terms of person-to-person transmission. The Eton College results imply that the school was hit vertically by the influenza virus during the night hours, or possibly at a weekend, and that the vertical incidence was patchy enough to distinguish between the locations of the various houses, some of which happened to lie in safe areas and others in dangerous areas. Dr Briscoe informed us that there had been a similar pattern in other influenza epidemics, except that the identities of the lucky and unlucky houses had been different. A patchy distribution in the incidence of the influenza virus at ground-level resulting from the fine details of how raindrops evaporated at the end of a shower would of course not be reproducible from one epidemic to another.

Further evidence against the standard dogmas of influenza transmission comes from an analysis of influenza in Japan. Several of Japan's prefectures (administrative regions) have population densities well in excess of 2000 per square kilometre, whereas others have less than 200 per square kilometre. Figure 11.9 shows the attack rates of influenza by prefecture, plotted against population density. If standard theories were valid, one would expect a clear rise of attack rate with increasing population density. No such effect is seen. Table 11.1 gives the incidence rates in a number of prefectures for five different years. The great degree of patchiness seen here further supports the theory that the infall of the virus is controlled by meteorological factors. The results in both Figure 11.8 and Table 11.1 are inconsistent with an infective model and show that attack rates are determined by the location of a school or an area in relation to an infall pattern which is patchy over a distance scale ranging from 100 metres to 100 kilometres.

In general, it is easier to test the theory of the atmospheric incidence of bacteria and viruses from the data for viral diseases, but in one case at least a bacterial disease appears to be of great interest, especially as it would seem to point to an explicit cometary source for the bacteria in question. It has long been known that whooping cough occurs in a cycle of 3.4–3.5 years, which used to be explained in terms of what was called the 'density of susceptibles' theory. The idea was that, after children susceptible to the disease become exhausted by a particular epidemic, it took about three-and-a-half years for new births to rebuild the density of susceptibles to the level at which a further epidemic could run. According to this theory, the periodicity should have been a function of population density, the shortest periods being found in inner-city areas of very high density, and either long periods

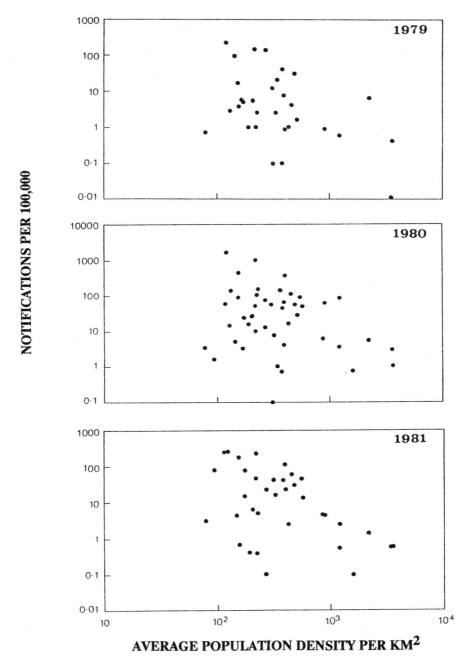

Figure 11.9 Notifications of influenza A in the prefectures of Japan plotted against average population density.

Table 11.1 NOTIFICATIONS OF INFLUENZA BY PREFECTURE PER 100,000 POPULATION.

Prefecture number	Average population density per square kilometre	1970	1977	1979	1980	1981
8	423	6.6	61.4	1.0	16.8	2.5
11	1580	114.4	1.4	–	0.8	0.1
12	869	37.4	5.5	–	6.4	4.2
13	3600	63.4	2.8	0.4	1.1	0.6
14	2197	51.7	20.5	6.7	5.7	1.4
15	205	113.3	2.0	5.4	25.2	6.3
16	225	67.5	312.1	2.5	101.6	4.9
17	217	399.7	95.9	139.1	10.8	0.4
18	117	375.5	2750.4	–	57.1	264.4
19	189	126.0	19.1	1.0	16.5	0.4
20	165	5.6	49.7	5.9	3.5	–

Source: Annual data from Japanese health authorities.

or no periodicity at all in lightly populated rural areas. But the periodicity, in Britain at any rate, was found to be everywhere the same, in town and country alike, in sharp contradiction with the theory – which should evidently have been abandoned immediately. Instead it has been propagated in the education system for nearly a century. Figure 11.10 shows the record of whooping-cough notifications for the period 1940–82. Had this theory been correct, the sudden reduction in the density of susceptible children brought about in the 1950s by the introduction of an effective vaccine should have greatly disturbed the periodicity, or even destroyed it altogether. Yet the periodicity persisted exactly as before, but with the total number of cases greatly reduced. The data in Figure 11.10 provide clear evidence of an externally forced periodicity of the kind that would arise if the *pertussis* bacterium (which causes whooping cough) arrived on the Earth from outside at regular intervals. With the possibility of a cometary connection in mind, the culprit can hardly fail to be Comet Encke. It is known that small particles associated with Comet

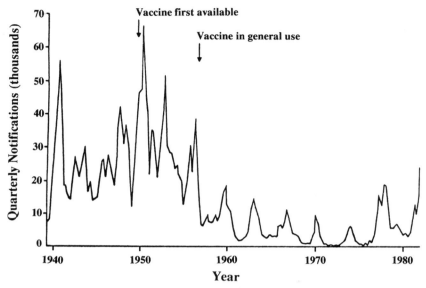

Figure 11.10 Whooping-cough notifications in England and Wales for the period 1940–82.

Encke enter the Earth's atmosphere. The particles, with sizes of the order of a millimetre, are destroyed by friction in the atmosphere, leaving luminous trails that form meteor showers: the Beta Taurids from 23 June to 7 July, and the Alpha Taurids from 20 October to 25 November, these being the times of the year when the Earth passes through the streams of debris deposited by Comet Encke. These streams are shown in Figure 11.11, projected onto the plane of the Earth's orbit.

Comet Encke is unusual among comets in having the whole of its orbit inside that of Jupiter, a feature which demands an exceptional history involving a near-encounter with one of the inner planets as well as an encounter with Jupiter, and possibly also one with Neptune. This history makes it likely that the present comet is no more than a fragment of the original body, and indeed the debris of the Taurid streams shown in Figure 11.11 represent other smaller fragments. It has been suggested, in particular by Victor Clube and Bill Napier, that the original comet was exceptionally large and that among the

123

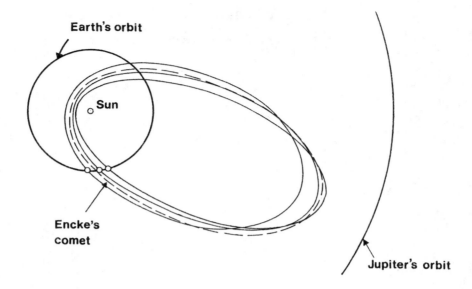

Earth's orbit

Sun

Encke's comet

Jupiter's orbit

Figure 11.11 The orbits of debris from three large fragments of Comet Encke which intersect the Earth's orbit at the points marked. There has been some perturbation of these streams away from the orbit of the comet itself (the dashed line), with corresponding small changes in period.

debris were many pieces not much smaller than Comet Encke itself. One fragment from the comet may have struck the Earth in recent times, as we shall see in Chapter 13.

When a larger body breaks up into a number of smaller ones the orbits of the fragments are all initially much the same. But because their close approaches to Jupiter occur at somewhat different times and in somewhat different configurations, their orbits diverge one from another more and more as time goes on. Figure 11.11 shows how the projections of the orbits of three separate fragments onto the plane of the Earth's orbit have diverged. Although the original comet may not have been in an orbit which intersected the Earth's orbit exactly, some of the fragments have come to possess this special property through the perturbation of their orbits by the gravitational pull of Jupiter.

Now, divergence is particularly effective in generating Earth-crossing orbits when the period of revolution of a fragment around the Sun happens to be an exact fraction of the orbital period of Jupiter, 11.86 years. Thus, for example, fragments with an orbital period equal to two-sevenths of 11.86 years could develop variations large enough to produce changes from an orbit that initially missed the Earth by a considerable margin, as Comet Encke does, to one that intersected the Earth's orbit exactly. Now, two-sevenths of 11.86 years is 3.39 years, which is close to the periodicity of whooping cough shown in Figure 11.10 (remembering also that there is a spread of about a year in the time of the fall of bacteria through the Earth's atmosphere). This is suggestive and, we think, interesting.

If these considerations are correct, there would be a strong motive to send a spacecraft to Comet Encke. The comet is reachable at all times. Even at its greatest distance from the Sun, aphelion, it is nearer to us than to Jupiter. At aphelion its speed is low, about a tenth of the speeds involved in the recent encounter with Comet Halley. Partly for this reason, and partly because Encke ejects dust less copiously than Comet Halley, there should be little danger from dust bombardment in taking a space probe close to Encke. We do not think it would require much, if any, advance on present-day technology to make an actual landing on the comet, to scoop up samples of material and then to return to Earth. (Indeed, there have been plans for precisely such a recovery, including a proposed European Space Agency mission called Rosetta, but whether they come to anything remains to be seen.) If the whooping-cough bacterium does come from Comet Encke, then so, in all likelihood, do other pathogens, including viruses. Encke was at perihelion, and therefore fairly close to the Earth, in 1918, 1947, 1957, 1967 and 1977, all years in which the influenza virus is known to have undergone major shifts.

The possibility that pathogens might be recovered from their source(s) raises the interesting idea that, if they were recovered ahead of their arrival on Earth, the way would be opened for preparing preventative vaccines ahead of their requirement. Indeed, the whole of preventive medicine would be revolutionized.

Apart from its dark-hued military applications, space research has hitherto been not much more than a succession of devices designed to attract popular attention. The determining factor for lunar landings was not science, but how long the public would remain interested; once the public began to yawn, the landings were abandoned. Since then we have had unmanned landings on Venus and Mars, and flybys of the planets Jupiter, Saturn, Uranus and Neptune. Nothing except military applications has had a momentum of its own. But if the above ideas are right – and the evidence shown in Figures 11.9, 11.10 and 11.11 suggest there is a good chance that they are – then space research would have a strong ongoing motivation, a positive motivation far superior to the wholly negative military motivation. For the first time in human history the way may be opening for us to protect ourselves against the ravages of disease. Instead of passively waiting for diseases that would otherwise be unavoidable to strike, and then attempting to moderate their impact as much as possible, we have the opportunity to attack diseases at their source.

CHAPTER TWELVE

How much of evolution has really happened

It was unfortunate that the genuinely difficult problem of the origin and evolution of living organisms became bound up in the nineteenth century with a cultural struggle which, being a human affair, had no relation at all with the world of objective scientific reality. It was because Darwin's book the *Origin of Species* came to be regarded as the declaration of war between a new culture and the old Judaeo-Christian culture, with science, industrialism and socialistic concepts of the organization of society as its main threads, that the book became historically famous, rather than because it contained anything new. In fact, the *Origin of Species* was put together very largely from the already published work of other men, its subsequent fame resting far more on liberalistic thinking than on its original scientific content. From the *Life and Letters* of Thomas Henry Huxley, it is clear that he saw the great issue of the last decades of the nineteenth century to be one of replacing prevailing Judaeo-Christian dogma with new ideas. There was hardly any examination at all of the relevant scientific questions and problems by those who became embroiled in an acrimonious battle between church and science. Every scientific issue was dealt with by the claim that the answers were all 'in Darwin', a kind of scientific fundamentalism not greatly different in its philosophy from that we associate today with religious fundamentalism. All hope of improving our understanding of the origin and evolution of living organisms thus became blocked, and it is quite likely to remain so for some time to come because of the extent to which it has become diffused throughout the education system.

Long before Darwin, naturalists concerned with the classification of plants and animals according to their structural forms had noticed marked similarities, such as the mechanical arrangement of bones in the limbs of animals, which clearly pointed to connections between widely separated classes, as for instance between reptiles and mammals. The problem was to explain how the connections had come about. One possibility was through evolution from a common source, so that descendants would possess at least some of the properties of their distant ancestor no matter how diverse in their forms they might become. Another perfectly valid possibility is that plants and animals are built from a number of genetic subroutines, in which case morphological, or body-plan, similarities would imply the use and adaptation of the same subroutines, without evolutionary connection being necessary. Just what evolution there had been would then remain an open question. Without a knowledge of modern genetics it was impossible in the nineteenth century to formulate this second possibility in a scientific way, which is to say in a way that could be developed through observation and experiment. The second possibility had therefore to be formulated in a religious way, religion providing a means of expressing and making use of ideas before their time is really due. What was said was that God had created species. If it suited Him to create plants and animals with morphological similarities, as for instance the similar mechanical arrangement of bones in the limbs of reptiles and mammals, then so be it – amen, nothing more to be said. 'Amen', the device that God is so omnipotent that no further questions are permitted, worked for many centuries, but by the latter half of the nineteenth century it would work no longer. With the power of monarchies in decline all over Europe, the concept of omnipotence was on its way out, a process which has been fully completed in our own times due to the most amazing phenomenon in all of social history: the emergence of TV interviewers before whom heads of states are humbled on a daily basis – and before whom, one feels, even the Roman emperors would have wilted. At all events, substitute genetic subroutines arriving on Earth from outside for God, and the second possibility becomes just as logically acceptable as the evolutionary possibility. The issue is then to balance the two, perhaps with the further possibility of their turning out not to be as mutually exclusive as the cultural battle of the nineteenth century made them appear to be.

Once the similarities of structure, which are undoubtedly present among plants and animals, were interpreted according to evolution, the classification scheme which had been arrived at empirically by naturalists became translated into an evolutionary scheme, an evolutionary scheme that was given a clear pictorial form by the analogy of a branching tree. The tree has a primordial trunk, rooted, Darwin suggested, in some little pond with all sorts of phosphoric salts, a suggestion which in our century became translated into the brew of 'organic soup' discussed in Chapter 3. The primordial trunk of the tree of life was then considered to fork into a number of major first-order branches, designated kingdoms by the classificationists. Thereafter each first-order branch forked into a number of second-order branches known as phyla or divisions. Each of these forked into third-order branches called classes, which in turn forked into fourth-order branches – orders. Then fifth-order branches, families; sixth-order branches, genera; and finally seventh-order twigs – species.

It may be wondered why there is so much emphasis in biology on species. Why the *Origin of Species*, when species according to the classification scheme are only seventh-order twigs? Why not the *Origin of Orders*, or the *Origin of Classes*? Part of the answer is that most of the explicit evidence for evolution was at the level of species, among the small shoots and twigs of the tree. The other part of the answer is that, to a good approximation, species defined the level in the classification scheme at which the interbreeding of organisms is possible. Broadly speaking, an organism propagates in one of four ways. Unisexual single-celled organisms propagate by fission or by budding, 'cloning' as we would say nowadays. Organisms with two distinct sets of genes, two sexes, may still propagate by cloning, parthenogenically with one or other of the sexes reproducing by itself; or each individual organism may contain both sexes, hermaphrodites; or, as in the higher animals, the sexes may be distinct and reproduction may depend on a combination of genes, one set female, the other male. Sustained reproduction from generation to generation then depends crucially on the two sets of genes being closely similar to each other. Sets of genes which are only moderately similar will not work. It is at the species level, the seventh-order branches, where it is determined whether the similarity is sufficient for interbreeding to occur, and this is why so much emphasis is given to species.

It can be demonstrated mathematically that the system of sexual mating, involving a process known as crossover which is responsible for the need of male and female genes to match each other closely, is essential if organisms with many genes are to avoid serious degeneration from one generation to the next. Indeed, it can be proved that the number of genes we actually possess is just of the order that it is possible to protect from degeneration with the aid of the sexual system. This is why organisms that normally propagate parthenogenetically or hermaphroditically nevertheless go into distinct sexually propagated generations from time to time, thereby again establishing sharp distinctions between species also for them.

The distinctness of species seemed a big point to the creationists, who argued that God had made it so, thereby giving to each of His creations a separate recognizable identity. To the question of why God had then made so many instances of species that were nearly the same, there was of course no answer, because by the rules of religions one is not permitted to ask questions about the motives of God. So, by the characteristic device of blocking valid questions the creationists ran themselves into trouble. It is all very well to pay attention to circumstantial evidence in science provided one asks every reasonable question one can, and provided all the circumstantial evidence points in the same direction. But to choose whatever may happen to suit your case while blocking the rest is asking for trouble, and so it has proved for the creationists, since with the coming of genetics there is now a clear and rational explanation of why species are distinct.

The mistake of the Darwinians, on the other hand, has been to think that by knocking out the creationists their case became proven, as if science were a contest between humans, like a sporting event. If science is to be thought of as a contest, then it is against the Universe, not against humans. Disposing of the views of someone else does no good at all towards establishing the truth of your own views, a lesson the Darwinians have never managed to learn.

The distinctness of species appeared to force evolution to occur in very small steps, for if a sudden big mutation occurs only as an unlikely event in any generation, there will be no possibility in a sexual system of the exceptional changed individual finding a partner with whom mating can take place successfully. Thus only changes within the bounds of a species could be contemplated, only new varieties within species could arise – tiny new shoots on the tree of life at an eighth order of refinement. For such shoots to become seventh-order twigs, then sixth-order branches, and so on, a great many other twigs and branches had to fall off the tree: many species, genera, families had to become extinct, thereby forcing the process to be extremely slow. *Natura non facit saltum*, Darwin always insisted, 'Nature does not go in jumps'. But in that case there would also be plenty of time for the process to be captured in the fossil record, the history of the ever-changing tree being faithfully recorded as sedimentary rocks were laid down and living organisms occasionally became buried in accumulating muddy debris.

The quantity of sediments laid down along the continental margins has been immense in almost every geological period, amounting in most cases to depths of several kilometres, indeed to the amounts of exposed rock that we can see in high mountain ranges or excavated by rivers into immense gorges like the Grand Canyon. The amount of sedimentary rock distributed all over the Earth, with rocks exposed somewhere or other from essentially all geological epochs going back in time to the beginning of organized forms of life some 600 million years ago, is indeed so great that one would think it highly favourable for the fossil record to reveal even the rather fine details of the evolution of the tree of life, at any rate of those parts of the tree bearing marine organisms. Yet this has not been the case, as critics among geologists were already pointing out in 1860, immediately after the publication of the *Origin of Species*. Critics were brushed aside by the Darwinians with the argument that, despite the efforts of geologists, the picture in 1860 was still very incomplete. So the

Darwinians were eating their cake and keeping it. Evolution was to be slow enough to meet the biological requirements, but not slow enough to have been captured in the fossil record. Experience shows that this style of thinking is inherently dangerous in that it leads all too easily to serious mistakes. By coming to think in the same fashion as the creationists whom they affected to despise, the Darwinians rested easy in their consciences. Evolution according to Darwinism was right, a view not to be questioned; this became the primary axiom of biological thinking. Anything required to make Earth-centred Darwinism seem to work had also to be correct, as for example the incompleteness of the fossil record. The fossil record had to be incomplete, otherwise Darwinism would be wrong, which was unthinkable – after all, if Darwinism were not right, what else could there be? Nothing. Therefore, again, case proven. It has been this flawed mode of thought that has dominated the biological sciences for more than a century, predictably with the unfortunate results we have referred to before.

One could make a case that, following the publication of the *Origin of Species*, the situation should have been allowed to run for a while to see how, with increasing geological knowledge, things would develop. In Chapter 7 we described how a sequence of fossil horses became regarded as lending strong support to the evolutionary theory; but, as the old saying has it, one swallow does not make a summer. Always in science it is the momentum of discovery that gives the best indication of the correctness or otherwise of a theory. Fossil horses were actually known a decade before the publication of the *Origin of Species*, so the situation as it developed in the 1870s was not really new. It is only what is really new that carries weight following the announcement of a theory. It is all too easy to construct theories to fit already-known facts and thereafter to show pre-adjusted agreements as apparent support for such theories. Such agreements are clearly not impressive at all. It is when one does not know a result beforehand, as with the infrared measurements discussed in Chapter 4, that one must pay serious attention to a theory.

So how has the situation turned out over the past century, as a veritable army of geologists have examined exposed rock sequences from all over the world? It has turned out no different from what was known already at the time of publication of the *Origin of Species*. Not only does the supposed evolutionary tree of life have no proper roots in some 'little pond' full of all manner of phosphoric salts, but it has no primary trunk. No connections have been found between first-order branches (kingdoms) and second-order branches (divisions or phyla). Nor have connections been found between second-order branches and third-order branches (classes), or with fourth-order branches (orders). Some connections may exist between fourth and fifth-order branches (families), although the botanist J. C. Willis denied that any existed for plants. According to Willis, it is only when one comes to sixth-order branches (genera) that connections with fifth-order branches (families) appear to exist. Even this limited success for the evolutionary theory is tempered, however, by connections not being gradual, as they were supposed to be: *natura facit saltum*, rather than Darwin's *natura non facit saltum*. Branchings appear to be sudden, as is shown in Figure 12.1, which illustrates the evolutionary sequence for the orders of mammals. It will be seen that many orders of mammals are supposed to have diverged from an ancestral stock which had developed before the remarkable extinctions of 65 million years ago, at the end of the Cretaceous geological period, extinctions which are said to have wiped out about a half of all the genera of animals, including most of the dinosaurs. The ancestral stock of the mammals lived through this traumatic episode, not long afterwards splintering into the many orders shown in Figure 12.1, a process indicated by broken lines which are conjectural, not actually found in the fossil record.

The problem for the Darwinian theory can be illustrated by considering just two of the orders shown in Figure 12.1, and two families within them: bears (family Ursidae, in order Carnivora) and of horses (family Equidae, in order Perissodactyla). It is surely reasonable to suppose that it takes more evolutionary steps to produce the difference between bears and horses than it takes to produce the comparatively minor changes among horses that were emphasized so strongly in the 1870s, or to produce comparatively minor changes among bears. So, if everything in evolution happens in small steps as Darwin claimed, it should have taken much longer to produce the divergence between orders, for example between bears and horses,

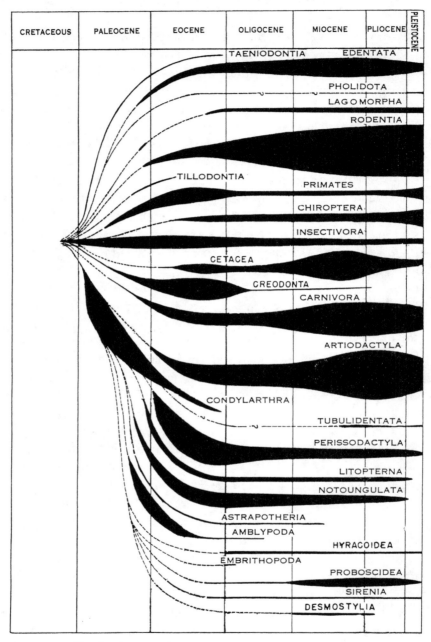

Figure 12.1 The fossil record for the orders of mammals is shown by the solid areas, the dotted continuations being only conjectural. The widths of the solid strips indicate changing numbers of species in the various orders.

than to produce subsequent minor changes. Hence, sampling the fossil record at more or less random moments in the evolutionary process should have turned up far more evidence of the big divergences than of the small ones. But the evidence is the other way round, and it is the other way round for all classes of animals, not just mammals: the small divergences are there, the big are absent. We do not see part-bear, part-horse. Even within a single order, families remain stubbornly distinct from one another. For instance, the order Carnivora includes cats and dogs, and it is obvious that we see no evidence whatsoever of part-cat, part-dog. Bears are always obstinately bears and horses are always obstinately horses. If the evolutionary picture shown in Figure 12.1 is correct, then the big step, the splitting of the ancestral line into many orders, occurred so rapidly on a geological timescale that the fossil record was unable to capture it. If one accepts evolution, then the conclusion is that the tree of life must grow in huge spurts. Such a conclusion raises the problem of how such jumps could possibly occur, in view of the need for the male and female genetic structures to match each other closely. How could considerable jumps, which surely must be unlikely, occur in just the same forms to males and females simultaneously?

This by no means exhausts the list of problems. Many species, particularly among invertebrates, have no ancestral branches in the fossil record at all. There appears in those cases to have been very little evolution. Tiny shrimps have been found dating back 500 million years in the fossil record that are essentially identical to present-day shrimps. As far as the record for mayflies and dragonflies goes back, about 250 million years, the same is true, as it is for many other species of insects including bees (where, however, the record goes back only about 25 million years). Nor are these a small minority. Because the number of invertebrate species is comparatively vast, one can say that the great majority of terrestrial species show little demonstrable evidence of ever having undergone an appreciable degree of evolution. Most species appear suddenly in the fossil record, and from their first appearance to the present day they have remained essentially unchanged. Those species for which there has very likely been appreciable change, as for instance from fish through amphibians to reptiles and mammals, are really in the minority.

Tiny, single-celled algae called diatoms are a remarkable example, giving we think a clear-cut disproof of the usual evolutionary theory. The membranes of diatoms are built from a siliceous material often arranged in beautiful coloured patterns which have long been a delight to microscopists. Because such material is extremely durable (which is presumably why diatoms use it), and because diatoms exist in enormous numbers (about one-quarter of the Earth's atmospheric oxygen is due to the activity of diatoms) they are common in the fossil record. Consequently, diatoms should provide an excellent way for testing the usual evolutionary theory, with evolution to present-day diatoms marked by many clearly demarcated steps. But again, this is not what is found. As with shrimps, mayflies, dragonflies, cockroaches, scorpions and bees, diatoms appeared suddenly in the record about 100 million years ago, and they appeared complete in all their present-day perfection of forms and colours. We see no way in which these facts about diatoms, or indeed any of the facts described above, can be fitted into the Earth-centred Darwinian theory, whose adherents deal with the facts by ignoring them, a trait they are quick to condemn in creationists when the latter ignore facts about the age of the Earth.

The only respect in which the fossil record gives comfort to Darwinians is at the sixth- and seventh-order branchings, which is to say for genera and species. This, of course, is just the place from which the theory started out. When a theory is formulated to take account of certain already-known facts, the correspondence of the theory to those facts has a deliberately arranged quality about it, and so does not count very much in its favour. It is to further correspondences with initially unknown facts that one looks to give real weight to a theory. If no more are found, or if such new facts as appear go against the theory, the correct course should be to abandon it.

In any case, from the discussion in Chapter 6 we understand why it is that the Darwinian theory works at the very outer edges of the supposed evolutionary tree. It is because genes can be put out of action rather easily by internally generated mistakes in reproducing the genetic structure of a species from parents to offspring. It is also possible for genes which have barely gone out of action to be recovered spontaneously. This ability to put out of action and then recover properties according to the fluctuating demands of the environment explains the evolutionary adjustments that go on all the time, and in a profusion of detail, at the outer boundary of the tree. But branchings such as those illustrated in Figure 12.2 demand an acquisition of important new properties, and these cannot be explained by internally generated changes. We shall consider in the next chapter both this problem, and that of the mysterious unchanging forms of shrimps, dragonflies, diatoms, and so on and we shall see that these life-forms appear to constitute what previously we have called subroutines, but subroutines occurring on a grand scale.

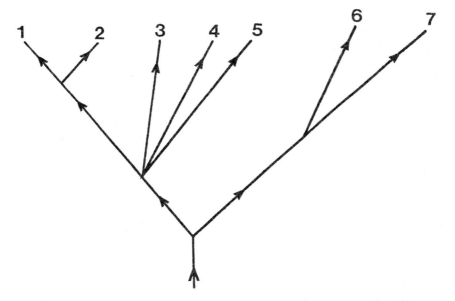

Figure 12.2 A so-called cladogram showing evolution by sudden jumps, the time sequence from generation to generation being indicated by the arrows.

Technical Note

Attempts have been made to construct an evolutionary tree of life by a means quite independent of the fossil record. Some of the biochemical substances produced by our genes are common to organisms in general, and have to do with processes basic to all life. An example is the process of electron transfer, in which about 20 substances known as cytochromes are involved. The third in order of their function, cytochrome-c, is simpler than others and has been much studied in order to establish the nature of the amino-acids which make up a chain of 102 links to yield the structure of cytochrome-c. Some 35 amino-acid links are found on careful examination of the chains for very different organisms to be always the same. About 25 other links vary only a little, while some 40 links are found to vary considerably among organisms as diverse as yeasts, plants, fish, amphibians, insects, reptiles and mammals.

By making the two assumptions (1) that there is a tree of life; and (2) that the considerably variable links have zero selective value; it is possible to use these data to construct a supposed tree of life. Trees can also be constructed for other important biosubstances in a similar way. The need to make the first of the above assumptions arises because, even if there were no tree, even if the variability of cyto-chrome-c occurred from species to species more or less at random, it would still be possible to construct some form of tree by this method. But then there would be no expectation that the resulting tree would bear any relation to the one obtained from classification according to the structural details of plants and animals. While these so-called phylogenetic trees obtained from studying substances like cytochrome-c prove to contain a few minor surprises, they do agree generally with what would be expected from old-style classification, indeed from pre-Darwinian classification dating back to the 1850s or even earlier. So the position is generally consistent, although because of the need for beginning by assuming the answer there can be no strict logical proof of evolution by this method.

The main objection, however, is to the second assumption. With some 60 per cent of the amino acids in the cytochrome-c chain invariant or nearly invariant, it is quite artificial to assume that the remaining 40 per cent are entirely free with zero selective value. Such an assumption is most unlikely to be true. It needs only a slight selective preference for one amino acid over another, a preference say of one part in ten thousand, for the preferred form to be adopted, a result which can readily be demonstrated mathematically. Now, what happens to be the preferred detailed structure for cytochrome-c in yeast, in fish, in mammals, is not likely to be the same to within margins as small as one part in ten thousand. So variability in cytochrome-c in the 40 per cent of amino acids on which the supposed tree is based is likely to be a consequence of function, with plants being slightly better served by one form and animals by another, sea-creatures being slightly different from land animals, reptiles slightly different from mammals, and so on. The deduced tree is therefore likely to be no more than a statement of similarities of function, which would not be expected to be much different from a statement of morphological similarities. The general correspondence of phylogenetic trees to classification trees is therefore to be expected, and just as a classification tree does not necessarily imply an evolutionary tree, neither do phylogenetic trees. The only evidence that would demand an evolutionary tree would be its explicit presence in the fossil record, and it is in fact notably absent, as we have seen above. What we may well be seeing in both phylogenetic trees and classification trees are organisms put together from similar components, similar subroutines, with those aggregates of components that are most similar simply being grouped together.

CHAPTER THIRTEEN

The subroutine problem

Viruses have all the properties needed for them to serve as the vehicle of evolution. In his book *The Common Cold*, Sir Christopher Andrewes describes the normal relation of a virus to its host cell in the following graphic terms:

What happens when a virus infects a cell is probably something like this. The protein part of a virus makes specific contact with something on the cell-surface. Then the cell ingests or takes the virus up within itself. It may ingest the whole virus and break it up inside, or, as happens with the bacteriophages or viruses infecting bacteria, the protein coat of the virus may be left outside the cell, only the essential nucleic acid gaining access to the interior. In either event, the protein part of the virus is expendable and plays no further part. The nucleic acid part, however, proceeds to instruct the cellular mechanism in a sinister manner. Suppose it is a rhinovirus infecting a cell lining your nose. The instruction will run thus: 'Stop making the ingredients necessary for making more nose-cells. Henceforth use your chemical laboratory facilities for making more nucleic acid like me.' The intruding virus nucleic acid gives the further instruction: 'And now make a lot of protein of such-and-such composition which I require wherewith to coat myself.' The cell can do nothing but obey and as more new virus particles are thus assembled by the cell's chemical mechanisms they are, at the end of the production-line, turned out into the outside of the cell. With many viruses, including probably rhinoviruses, the final effect is to exhaust the cell altogether, so that after a while it dies and disintegrates. The virus set free will infect more of its victim's cells until such time as defence mechanisms have been mobilized. It will also get into the outside world and infect more victims, for one result of the cell-destruction in the course of a cold infection will be inflammation, pouring out of fluid, sneezing and spread of virus. All of it a very conveniently organized affair for the benefit of rhinoviruses. (p. 24)

This may be true of the rhinovirus, the common-cold virus, yet other viruses have the well-proven ability in some cases of not destroying host cells but of developing a symbiotic relation with them. In some such cases the viral genetic material is actually known to add itself to the host genetic material, inevitably contributing several new genes at one fell swoop. So the process we are discussing quite certainly exists. What presumably happens is that a species which is persistently attacked over a long period by a particular virus gradually develops immunity to that virus, which is then forced into an increasingly passive role, to be eventually restricted in its multiplication to the natural division of the cell itself – in other words, it multiplies only with the cell, just like all other genetic material.

We can list the properties of viruses:

1 They carry genes, 'subroutines' in our computer analogy, and not all such genes are directed towards the replication process described above. Some appear to be just there, seemingly doing nothing as far as the virus itself is concerned. These conceivably might carry the subroutines required for evolution.
2 Viruses can add themselves to the normal genetic material of a cell, thereby adding a subroutine or subroutines.
3 Viruses can interfere with the normal 'running program' of a cell, with the possibility of changing the program so as to incorporate a new subroutine which it has brought, or even directing the cell to take a number of accumulated subroutines into its program. In short, what a virus can do is analogous to what a human

programmer does when adding a new subroutine to a computer program.

The difference is that a human programmer succeeds more often than a virus, although human programmers usually have to search around quite a bit before they achieve success. The process of disease is what we experience when attempted evolution fails, as it usually does. Yet even in defeat the process succeeds in one important respect: the virus is multiplied, so generating more of the basic components of life. Replication of viruses is necessary in order to make available an ample supply of subroutines, not just terrestrially but cosmically, although when we are suffering from a cold this particular advantage does not appear subjectively commendable to us.

A number of otherwise very puzzling points are cleared up immediately. Because of the ability of life-forms to replicate rapidly, be they plants or animals or microorganisms, evolution can well afford a large failure-to-success ratio. The rare success is hugely replicated, and so comes to outnumber the failures – indeed, only the successes are left in the end. Likewise we can expect only a minor fraction of the subroutines added to our cells to prove useful. More additions will be made than we use, so that the bulk of our genetic material at any time will have no utility, as is actually the case. It has been estimated that only about 5 per cent of our genetic material is currently functional.

It is easy now to see how evolution can go in jumps, an impossibility in the Darwinian theory (unless one makes the exceedingly unlikely assumption that every time a species makes a jump, its entire membership is cut down to a single pair of severely mutated identical twins). Evolution triggered by viruses can affect a substantial fraction of a population in the same way at the same time, just as in a worldwide pandemic. Large numbers of males and females would be equally affected, so that the genetic matching necessary for successful mating can be maintained, despite the genetic structures being appreciably changed. As in an epidemic of the common cold, the new species after an evolutionary jump consists of all those individuals who caught the cold, and the old species consists of all those who avoided the cold, only of course the situation would be vastly more severe than a common cold in those that were changed. Unlike the

Darwinian theory, with its dependence on minute internal mutations and so requiring the precept *natura non facit saltum*, evolution by viral addition positively requires evolution to go in jumps. A plant which acquires the ability to produce a new colour cannot produce half a colour, for example – the plant either acquires the gene to produce the colour or it does not. The situation is necessarily discrete, just as J. C. Willis, to explain his botanical observations, insisted it had to be.

In earlier chapters we have given strong evidence for regarding comets as the source of the microorganisms incident upon the Earth. The comets that contribute to the halo of small particles around the Earth are only a minority, however. Most of the comets in the so-called Oort Cloud around the Solar System, which extends outwards an appreciable fraction of the distance to the nearest star, remain in their remote orbits far from the inner regions of the Solar System, and so do not interact with the Earth. But from time to time a passing star or molecular cloud in the Milky Way will disturb the cometary cloud. A passing star travels at such high speed that the comets in the outer regions of the Oort Cloud scarcely move during such a passage. However, comets close to its path will have their motion perturbed by the gravitational pull of the star, and a modest fraction of the perturbations will have the effect of bringing comets in to the inner regions of the Solar System, where the heat of the Sun will persuade them to disgorge microorganisms and so contribute to the rain of viruses falling on to the Earth. Thus the cause of the rain of viruses is the passage of stars through the cometary cloud, or in exceptional situations the approach of the Solar System to a massive molecular cloud in the Milky Way.

Passage near a molecular cloud produces larger disturbances but occurs less frequently, perhaps once in 100 million years, whereas the penetration of the cometary cloud by a star occurs about once in a million years. The pattern is thus for a light but rather steady injection of comets to the inner regions of the Solar System occurring most of the time, as at present, but very occasionally, about once in 100 million years, for there to be a much larger sudden burst of incoming comets, and consequently for there to be a large cascade of viruses onto the Earth.

This astronomical expectation agrees very well with the evolutionary implication of the fossil record that the principal episodes of evolution occurred quickly, almost too quickly to be captured at all in their details, and in immense bursts at intervals of the order of a geological period, about 100 million years. According to our picture it is therefore the passage near a molecular cloud in the Milky Way that causes the occasional major bursts of evolution. Most of the time, as at present, the general distribution of plants and animals is only lightly disturbed, but from time to time there is an immense upheaval, causing major branching on the evolutionary tree.

Throughout our discussion, in this and previous chapters, we have mostly dealt with issues on a point-by-point basis, without seeking to strengthen one point by appealing to another. Yet every aspect of our eventual picture turns out to go in the same direction, towards life being external to the Earth, arriving on the Earth from the outside, and its subsequent development here being controlled, not from within terrestrial organisms themselves as the conventional Earth-centred biology of the nineteenth century assumed it to be, but from the outside. When one throws all the evidence we have discussed together, so that it is seen as a whole, the case for this cosmically oriented point of view becomes, we think, overwhelming. It is a further inevitable extension of the Copernican Revolution. All experience shows that it would simply not be possible for so many facts and arguments to be consistently successful if the picture were intrinsically wrong. The position we have reached seems secure enough for us to proceed to the more amazing aspects of it, with some assurance that we are on the right track. Otherwise one might all too easily be turned aside by the far-reaching implications of what has so far been discovered.

The sudden appearance about 100 million years ago of diatoms in the fossil record, already with wonderfully complex patterns in their siliceous cell membranes, suggest that diatoms arrived on the Earth from outside at that time. This view is supported by the existence of certain species of diatoms in the Arctic and Antarctic, without those species existing in the warmer temperate and tropical regions of the Earth, as if the connection between the polar regions was via the space outside the Earth, not by horizontal travel over the terrestrial surface.

If diatoms are taken to have arrived upon the Earth fully fledged in their intricate and beautiful structural forms, what are we to say of other creatures such as shrimps, mayflies, cockroaches . . .? Bees, even? Did they all arrive from outside? To the biologist educated according to conventional beliefs the idea of bees from space will seem preposterous. But why? By what mental process, except educational prejudice, can one make such a judgement? After all, the Universe is a much vaster place than the Earth, so it would seem a better bet in principle to opt for the Universe as a source of bees rather than the Earth – unless of course there is some demonstrable physical reason why such a hypothesis is impossible. At first sight, there does seem to be such a physical reason but on more considered examination the difficulty disappears, thereby giving the hypothesis an inverted kind of support – every challenge which an idea survives gives it a bit of extra status.

In this case, the obvious first objection one can make to multicelled animals, metazoans, arriving from space is that they could never manage to land safely. A lone bee coming at a speed in excess of 10 kilometres per second into the Earth's atmosphere, even into the tenuous high atmosphere, would unquestionably be converted into a puff of smoke. But a bee or other creature of comparable size embedded in a smallish body, say half a metre in diameter, could survive landing on the Earth provided the material of the body has suitable properties. The material would need to have sufficient strength for the bonds not to shatter under the pressure exerted on it by the atmosphere as it was slowed down to a modest speed, and its heat conductivity would have to be low enough for the heat generated at the surface of the body not to penetrate into the interior and cook the creature. Such a process would be similar to that which actually happens for meteorites, where the initial energy of motion goes into the evaporation of an outer shell, leaving an interior to fall quite slowly down to the ground, an interior which often remains cool. One could conceive of a metazoan landing inside a meteorite, although it would be better for the material of the parent body to become dispersed after reaching ground-level, thereby releasing any organisms it might have contained. This could happen if the material were organic, instead of being either metal or stone, as for meteorites.

Normally, comets are thought of as bodies about 5 kilometres in diameter, but it is certain that many bodies of a cometary kind exist that are appreciably smaller than visible comets like Comets Halley and Encke. This has been verified by keeping a close watch on the atmosphere of the Sun; smaller cometary bodies have been seen to evaporate there. A body now believed to have been a fragment of Comet Encke with a diameter of perhaps a hundred metres hit the Earth on 30 June 1908 near the Tunguska River in Siberia. It plunged through the atmosphere and exploded violently about 10 kilometres above the ground, leaving a scene of peculiar and extensive devastation. Trees were felled over thousands of square kilometres, and seismic waves, as if from an earthquake, were detected in Europe. The bodies, about a metre in size, which generated North and South Ray craters on the Moon (Chapter 9) were also very likely of a cometary nature. Indeed, for there to be a sufficient number of comparatively young craters in the size range from 10 to 100 metres for astronauts to have come on them in the limited areas of the Moon that were explored during the Apollo missions, it is necessary that a large number of bodies a metre or more in diameter be present in the cometary distribution. Comets may have been formed more or less as we see them, by condensation processes in the early history of the Solar System, or they may be fragmentation products from collisions between much larger bodies, bodies perhaps the size of the Moon, in which case fragmentation would produce all manner of sizes, almost surely with a vast number of small bodies being generated.

A body with a diameter of about a metre falling into the Earth's atmosphere on the night-side would produce a flash of light lasting half a minute or so, on a clear night appearing at least as bright as the full Moon, and visible from the ground over an area of a hundred kilometres or more across. One reads many accounts of bright flashes of light being seen, but it is hard to discover precisely what happened, if only because such matters touch security issues – the reader may possibly remember an intense flash of light seen in the South Atlantic that became widely discussed because it was claimed by some to be evidence of a nuclear-bomb test conducted by the South African government. Although statistics reported by meteor observers are directed to more frequent and much smaller events, they also indicate that very bright flashes occur from time to time, suggesting that bodies with sizes of the order of ten centimetres to a metre in diameter may well be incident on the Earth at a rate of a few per year. There is similar evidence from satellite observations, although again for security reasons it is difficult to know what should be trusted there and what not. One might further suspect that the reason why the UFO cult manages to persist is because there are enough genuine occurrences of unusual bright features in the story to provide a factual basis for the cult.

If small-sized bodies are regarded as fragments along with the usual comets from the break-up of larger bodies, their content with respect to bacteria and viruses should be the same. This would add an interesting further dimension to the discussions in Chapters 10 and 11. As well as pathogens being incident from a large halo of cometary debris enveloping the whole Earth, there could also be highly localized effects, in which a particular pathogen came to be distributed over an area with a diameter of only a few tens of kilo-metres. Instead of epidemics arising on an international scale as in worldwide pandemics, there would be an apparently mysterious outbreak at a particular locality, with nothing occurring outside the small area of incidence, and with the outbreak soon dying away as the pathogen became carried off into the sea or into a much larger area by streams and rivers, or buried in the soil or absorbed into the water table. Such highly localized outbursts do in fact occur, affecting both humans and other animals. In the past their limited impact caused them to come and go almost without general notice, but in these days of intense media coverage a notable localized outburst of some unexpected disease hits the headlines in a nation the size of Britain every year or two.

In one important respect the constraints on bringing a multicelled creature to the Earth are weaker than for the influenza virus. To explain the widespread contemporaneous occurrence of a particular disease, like that of the outbreak of the common cold studied by van

Loghem, it is necessary for very many viral particles to be incident on the Earth in just a few days. But many millions of years are available to only a few mating couples of metazoans to succeed in making an effective terrestrial landing. Such events need only be very rare. As long as they happen at all, the puzzle of the existence of so many non-evolving life-forms can be solved. Quite likely, the majority of life-forms that succeed in making a landing do not find the environment here to their liking, and so come to nothing. A big element of chance as to which life-forms succeed and which do not would be expected, perhaps with the situation changing as conditions change on the Earth. For example, one could imagine that flowering plants could not establish themselves until after insects became established. Very likely, a logical order of establishment would be dictated quite generally by ecological interactions, with the development of mammals perhaps being more dependent on the appearance of flowering plants than on the often-mentioned extinction of the dinosaurs.

It must be granted, then, that it would be possible for a biological system as large as an insect to land safely on the Earth; not insects in immense swarms, perhaps, but from time to time and in special circumstances, a few of them. Neither a bacterium nor a virus that manages to fit into the terrestrial environment has any problem about replication, but metazoans would have an insurmountable problem if their sexual patterns were like that of mammals. It would be necessary for a mammal to have both a male and a female incident on the Earth in the same place and at the same time. For humanoids who landed purposively in a spacecraft in the style recommended by Francis Crick and Leslie Orgel, the problem would not of course exist, since male and female humanoids would automatically be together by design. But for a male metazoan, with a very small chance of making a successful landing, the probability of there being also a female who made an independent successful landing at just the same time and place would be impossibly small. We can deduce, therefore, that sexual patterns in creatures landing from space need to be markedly different from the pattern of mammals. There are three workable alternatives, and it appears highly significant that each of the alternatives is actually represented among plants and simpler animals.

One possibility is for either sex to be able to reproduce by itself, a female for example reproducing a large number of other females, the process of parthogenesis possessed by most invertebrate species. A female landing successfully on the Earth would reproduce so as to generate a large number of similar cloned females who would then spread out to cover an appreciable area, an area into which a male eventually succeeding in making a landing would find females on hand for reproduction (or vice versa with respect to the sexes). If such a process were to continue for too many generations there would be serious genetic degeneration, but something of the order of ten thousand generations should be genetically sustainable, permitting a considerable interval of time for the incoming partner to arrive, and enabling the geographical target area over which the first arrival spreads to become considerable.

The second possibility is for each individual to contain both sexes. An individual then spreads hermaphroditically after making a successful landing, again establishing an appreciable target area into which later individuals can fall successfully, and genetically necessary crosses between individuals can then take place. This possibility exists characteristically for plants. The third possibility is for individuals to undergo a sexual cycle, an individual being male over part of the cycle and female over the rest of the cycle. As long as eggs from the female phase can persist until sperms become available from the male phase, this arrangement works like the hermaphroditic case. Shrimps are examples of creatures that undergo such sexual cycles.

It is interesting to consider the effect of reversing the above logic. Instead of arguing that plants and animals, in order to land successfully from outside the Earth, must possess one or other of these three sexual patterns, we can take the bold step of asserting that all organisms possessing one or other of these patterns arrived originally on the Earth from space, while those organisms which do not possess one of them have arisen by evolution. This step turns out to agree very well with the fossil record. It correctly distinguishes evolving lines from those showing little or no evolution.

How, the reader may ask, does 'Darwin's theory' explain the apparent oddities of these several different patterns of sexual behaviour? As primitive survivals. Survivals from what? From the environment as it used to be. What was this environment, then? Something which suited the several different sexual patterns, the triumphant Darwinian exclaims, going yet again around the well-loved tautological circle.

Having distinguished evolving lines from non-evolving lines using the fossil record, a prediction can be made. Evolving lines, according to the theory, must be susceptible to invasion by viruses. As far as we are aware, this is always true. What then about non-evolving lines? Since non-evolving lines are unaffected by viruses so far as evolution is concerned, we might risk the prediction that non-evolving lines do not interact with viruses as far as disease is concerned, either. In short, shrimps, cockroaches, mayflies, and so on should be free from viral diseases. After looking through extensive works on entomology, and after asking experts, we remain unsure of whether this general expectation is true or not. That the books say nothing, and that experts gaze in wonder on being asked the question, must mean that little is known, which in turn probably means that little in the way of viral diseases occur in such creatures, otherwise it would surely have been remarked upon at some length.

CHAPTER FOURTEEN

A summary of considerations necessary for understanding the origin and evolution of life

All of biology turns on the remarkable ability of biochemicals to speed up chemical reactions that otherwise take place only very slowly, in some cases speeding them up many billions of times. It is surprising that this should be possible at all, and the manner in which it is achieved is astonishing. The primary agent is the amino acid with the general chemical formula shown in Figure 14.1a, where R denotes any group of atoms that can link to the central carbon atom by a single covalent bond. In general, this permits there to be an immense number of amino acids, but in biology only 20 forms of R play a dominant role: R_1, R_2, ..., R_{20}, say. Figures 14.1b and c show how, by eliminating a water molecule, two amino acids are linked together by a so-called peptide bond. In this way, amino acids can become linked together into long chains, named polypeptides or proteins. A chain of 100 links would be considered rather short in biology. Yet with 20 possible choices for R at each link, the total number of chains with 100 links is 20^{100}, or 10^{130}, to the nearest order of magnitude. The longest protein chains run to about 2000 links, for which the number of possibilities is 20^{2000}, or about 10^{2600}, truly a big number. Journalists like to use the phrase 'astronomical numbers' for what they considered to be immensely large, but these numbers are 'super-

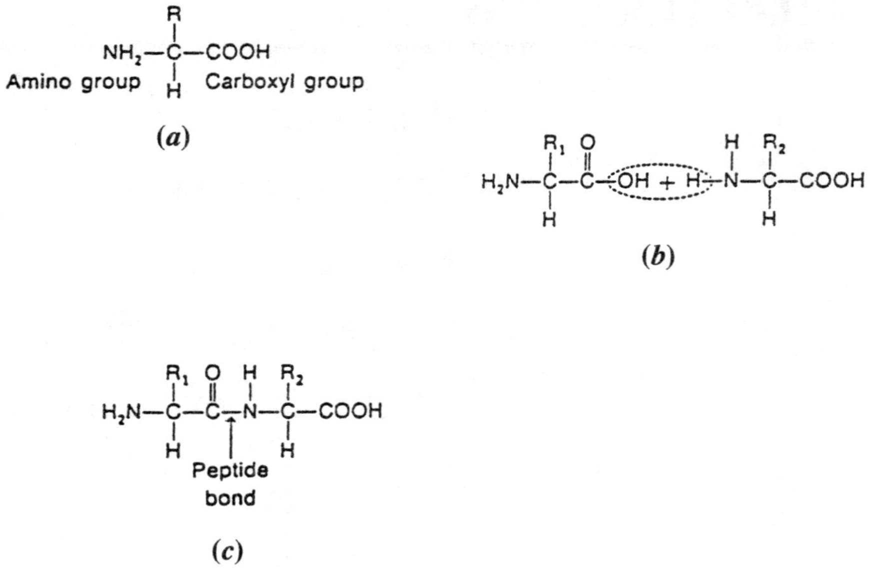

$$NH_2-\underset{\underset{H}{|}}{\overset{\overset{R}{|}}{C}}-COOH$$

Amino group   Carboxyl group

(*a*)

$$H_2N-\underset{\underset{H}{|}}{\overset{\overset{R_1}{|}}{C}}-\overset{\overset{O}{||}}{C}-OH + H-\underset{\underset{H}{|}}{\overset{\overset{H}{|}}{N}}-\underset{\underset{}{|}}{\overset{\overset{R_2}{|}}{C}}-COOH$$

(*b*)

$$H_2N-\underset{\underset{H}{|}}{\overset{\overset{R_1}{|}}{C}}-\overset{\overset{O}{||}}{C}-\underset{}{N}-\underset{\underset{H}{|}}{\overset{\overset{R_2}{|}}{C}}-COOH$$

Peptide
bond

(*c*)

Figure 14.1 Amino-acid structure and linkages: (*a*) the schematic structure of an amino acid; (*b*) to link two amino acids, a molecule of water is eliminated; (*c*) linked amino acids.

astronomical' in their largeness. Big numbers in astronomy usually have about 40 zeros, as have those in physics. Even the ratio of the largest distances in astronomy to the smallest lengths in physics has only about 60 zeros.

It is substances of this type which carry out the active chemical processes in our bodies. This is not done directly by genes. What genes do is to decide which among the immense super-astronomical number of possible amino-acid chains our bodies shall produce. The number actually produced is minute compared with the total number of possibilities, about 2000 in a simple bacterium and about 100,000 in a mammal. A major part of the problem of the origin of life is to understand how these highly restricted special choices came to be made, with particular emphasis on how it came about that the products chosen happen to possess astonishing catalytic properties, the ability to speed up otherwise very slow chemical reactions by factors of a billion or more.

The ability of a polypeptide to act as a catalyst turns critically on the three-dimensional shape into which the amino acid chain becomes curled when it is surrounded by water. Certain of the side groups R_1, R_2, and so on have the property of being repelled by water, and it is these hydrophobic forces which act as a first-order contribution in determining the three-dimensional shape of a polypeptide. What happens is that those amino acids with hydrophobic side groups get pushed towards the central region of the structure, and because the particular hydrophobic amino acids can be irregularly distributed along the chain, their being pushed towards the centre leads to a three-dimensional folding that is much more complex than a ball of wool. Parts of a polypeptide chain consisting usually of some five to ten sequentially connected amino acids may wind up on their own into a strand-like form. Using the convention that an arrow denotes a strand and a cylinder a helix, Figure 14.2 illustrates the complexities that arise when several amino-acid chains become linked together, as they sometimes do. The almost fantastic complexity of these structures is better shown when the shorthand of cylinders and arrows is not used, as in Figure 14.3, which shows the interlocking structure of the three polypeptide chains which form the substance alpha-chymotrypsin. Nor is even this the full measure of the complexity that is really involved. Since it may take years for biochemists to determine even one of these structures, it is natural for them to choose only the shorter polypeptide chains for study. Chains with up to 2000 amino acids must fold into structures still more complex.

Cysteine is one of the 20 biologically important amino acids, with the side group R equal to $-CH_2-SH$. The sulphur atom has the property of being able to bond strongly with another sulphur atom into a so-called disulphide bond. It happens that, in a curled-up structure like that shown in Figure 14.3, two cysteine members of the polypeptide, not adjacent at all to each other in the chain or chains, nevertheless come close enough to each other in the structure for a strong disulphide bond to become established between them. This acts as a stability point, giving firmness to the complex three-dimensional structure, the fine details of which are then determined by weak bondings between hydrogen atoms, by electrostatic forces and by van der Waals forces.

153

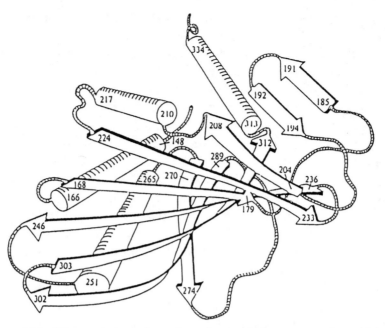

Figure 14.2 The catalytic region of a subunit of the enzyme glyceraldehyde-phosphate dehydrogenase. Helices are represented by cylinders, and strands by arrows. The numbers refer to locations on the polypeptide chain. (Adapted from *Journal of Biological Chemistry,* 1975, **250**, 9137–62.)

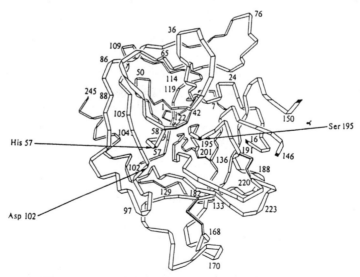

Figure 14.3 The structure of alpha-chemotoypsin, with three critical amino acids marked. The numbers refer to ordering of amino acids along the three chains which together constitute this enzyme. (Adapted from P. D. Boyer (ed.), *Enzymes*, 3rd edn, Vol. 3, Academic Press, New York, 1971.)

The enzymic ability of the resulting folded polypeptide, which is to say the ability to speed up greatly some particular chemical reaction, turns on its surface properties. A pocket at the surface must be capable of binding the reacting chemicals to itself so as to bring them not only into forcible contact with each other but also into an optimum orientation with respect to each other. And after the reaction has occurred the products must be released, freeing the enzyme to operate again, a necessary property of any catalyst. These requirements involve great complexities of shape and structure at the surface of the enzyme. This is illustrated by the well-known lock-and-key analogy shown in Figure 14.4, the intricate shape of the lock being intended to correspond to the complexities of shape at the surface pocket of the enzyme.

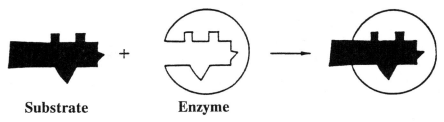

Substrate   **Enzyme**

Figure 14.4   Lock-and-key analogy for the operation of an enzyme, given in 1894 by Emil Fischer.

In their book *Fundamentals of Enzymology,* W. C. Price and L. Stevens remark: 'Enzymes display a number of remarkable properties when compared with other types of catalyst. The three most important are their high catalytic power, their specificity, and the extent to which their catalytic activity can be regulated by a number of naturally occurring compounds.' Only a very small fraction of all possible polypeptides display these properties for a particular chemical reaction or set of reactions, for example the set of reactions that release energy from sugars, a set that uses about thirty different enzymes, each one of which has a distinct highly specific function. Only those polypeptides that curl up so as to produce just the right kind of surface pocket to accommodate the so-called 'substrate' in a favourable way can promote catalytic action, and for this many conditions on how the 20 different amino acids are ordered along the polypeptide chain must be satisfied.

For proper enzymic function it is not sufficient to have just a short piece of the polypeptide chain right. Because the folding depends on the whole chain, and because the amino acids which form the surface pocket come from diverse places along the chain, the whole of it is involved. A polypeptide assembled from the 20 different kinds of amino acid by making a random choice for the identity of each link (i.e. a random choice of R at each link), and a random choice for the length of the chain, would be exceedingly unlikely to have the slightest enzymic ability with respect to the chemical reactions of importance in biology. Very many such random choices would have to be made before anything of relevance emerged. The number needed is indeed so large that it has not proved possible to determine it by direct experiment.

Some idea of how vast this number must be can be obtained indirectly, however, from restrictions on the variability of enzymes found among living organisms. A few enzymes are nearly invariant across the whole of biology, showing that essentially no change from a unique chain of amino acids has been permitted by natural selection. In other enzymes, amino-acid changes ('substitutions') are permitted, but not for all positions in the chain. Usually from about a third to a half of the amino acids are invariant. Every invariant amino acid contributes a factor of 20 to the estimate of how many attempts would be needed to discover the enzyme by a random assembly of amino acids. Thus, even for a short chain of 100 links of which 30 are invariant, we have 20^{30}, so that about 10^{39} attempts would have to be made before success was achieved. For an enzyme with 1000 links of which 300 are invariant, the required number of attempts is given by 20^{300} which is about 10^{390}. Evidently we are involved once again with super-astronomical numbers, especially as we are concerned not with a single enzyme but with 2000 different enzymes in even the simplest organisms, and with about 100,000 in complex creatures like ourselves.

How Earth-centred Darwinians imagine such numbers could be coped with in 'some little pond with all manner of phosphoric salts' defies the imagination. Before the complexities of modern microbiology had emerged, the mistake might be considered by the kind-hearted to be excusable, but nowadays the old belief of life emerging in Aristotelian fashion out of warm earth and morning dew, stirred together in some little pond, is not defensible. A strict logician might claim that it was not defensible even against the findings of Francesco Redi in the late seventeenth century, and certainly not against the work of Pasteur in the 1860s, for as Hermann von Helmholtz then put it:

> It appears to me that a fully correct scientific procedure, if all our attempts fail to cause the production of organisms from non-living matter, to raise the question whether life has ever arisen, whether it is not just as old as matter itself, and whether seeds have not been carried from one planet to another.

We can translate Helmholtz's statement into modern terms by saying that, since life involves super-astronomical numbers, it is useless to seek its origin in ordinary astronomical terms, useless to go from a little pond on the Earth to a pond in the Solar System, or even to a pond in our galaxy. The issue is one to be treated at a cosmological level, alongside such problems as the origin of the Universe.

Many biologists believe this to be a counsel of despair. They think one should persist with the little terrestrial pond in the distant hope of a simple solution somehow emerging. We think this point of view is similar to majority opinion as it existed in astronomy around the year AD 1600. Sixty years after Copernicus, most still held that the Earth was the centre of the Universe: it was only a handful of unorthodox philosophers and mathematicians who thought otherwise. An apparently respectable argument for the majority opinion was that, if the Earth were to be abandoned as a fixed rigid centre, then all manner of complications would be let loose – Pandora's box would be opened. And so it proved. Pandora's box was indeed opened, and still after almost four centuries we do not know what else might emerge from it. The ultimate problems today are just as unsolved as they were in AD 1600, and much more complex into the bargain. Yet nobody today thinks it was wrong to abandon the old Earth-centred ideas, even though in doing so scientists became committed to a path which continues to lead them into strange and difficult territory. In the years ahead the same is likely to happen with respect to the origin of life, as the problems there are pushed to more and more sophisticated levels. The Copernican Revolution is far from finished.

We live today in an age of instant solutions. Media penetration into science has demanded that everything, even the most important and profound issues, is presented as tiny packages that can be easily explained to a public which has made no study at all of the issues. Inevitably, this has led to an unpromising situation in which a measured approach to the solution of any difficult problem is submerged in the invention of catchwords and bogus concepts. The media have not the slightest interest in paths that will take centuries to explore. Yet it is in the nature of science that important issues almost always do take centuries to explore.

Although we cannot expect to solve the ultimate problem of the origin of life, given the correct path we can expect to solve many lesser problems, as for instance the arrival and development of life on the Earth. We have seen that viruses have the ability to enter the cells of evolving creatures such as ourselves, and having entered they disrupt and change the cell's internal processes. Often the disruptions lead to disturbances we call disease, which, if serious enough, can produce the death of a plant or animal. In other cases, however, the disruptions are sufficient to change the invaded organism – sometimes mildly, sometimes appreciably – without the changes being terminal. Viruses can add whole new genes not possessed previously by an organism, and very likely they can promote radical reorganizations of the whole of the genetic material within the cells of an organism. In view of the immense complexity of even a single gene, this should not surprise us; even a single gene can be thought of as possessing an immense information content, with intricate properties which it would take a whole library to describe.

Evolution by viral invasion solves problems that are insuperable for the biological theories of the nineteenth century. One of the major difficulties has been described already, but in view of its importance it is worth re-emphasizing. According to standard theory, mammals evolved from a reptilian branch called Synapsida. But the genetic material of a mammal is grossly different from that of a reptile. It is different in amount and it is quite different in its organization. To pass from one to the other would entail steps in which organizational structure was changed, for instance whole chromosomes would need to be changed. This sets the problem, for species which propagate by sexual reproduction, that a changed individual cannot mate successfully unless a member of the opposite sex can be found possessing almost exactly the same change. It is not sufficient to postulate an amazing feat of mis-copying that contrived to produce a highly beneficial structural change. We have to postulate the simultaneous occurrence of three miracles. Whatever miracle occurs to a male, say, there must be the even greater miracle that just the same structural change occurs, by a chance mis-copying, to a female, and furthermore, that the two miracles must happen in the same place at much the same time, otherwise the changed male will not find the changed female. Mathematically, this means that the probability of any appreciable change being successfully propagated is the product of three small numbers, making the result negligibly small.

Evolution by viral addition avoids this difficulty, because males and females can be similarly changed by the same externally imposed virus, and also with the possibility that the virus could be infectious from one individual to another, thereby changing simultaneously a considerable fraction of all the members of a species.

Another difficulty faced by nineteenth-century biology was to understand how the eye had appeared several times during the course of biological history, in such diverse creatures and at such times as to preclude there being any direct connection between the eyes of mammals or reptiles or fish, and those of the octopus and its relatives. Nor is any direct evolutionary connection possible between these cases and the compound eye of insects. Yet all three of these independent eyes function in basically the same way, on the change of shape of the same complex molecule. The natural explanation of this remarkable piece of evidence is that all eyes work on the same basic principle because they are all adaptations from a common source, not that they evolved independently of each other. Besides which, there are serious logical difficulties in trying to explain even one of the three cases according to nineteenth-century biological theory.

In Chapter 5 we saw how the optical system of a gull's eye is comparable in quality to the best man-made systems used nowadays in surveillance satellites, showing that the eyes of birds must possess corrections for spherical and chromatic aberrations, coma and astigmatism. How this came about is supposedly explained in biology by natural selection. In a fixed environment natural selection operates in a species to prevent adaptation to the environment from becoming worse, because defective individuals are selected against in the competition for survival. Most critics of the theory have been inclined to accept this statement as plausible, although it is easy to see that if strict mathematical standards were adopted the logic would have to be rejected, even at this first stage. Humans have lost the ability to synthesize vitamins, which is an example of a disadaptation to the environment.

However, if steps backward are excluded, then the only steps which can be made must be forward. But will any steps at all be made? The answer must be yes, because no material system can be copied a very large number of times without occasional mis-copying occurring. Overwhelmingly, most mis-copyings will be steps backward, but with steps backward excluded, steps are restricted to the occasional forward ones. So where does this leave us? Nowhere at all, really. There is nothing in the logic to tell us whether the steps forward will be sufficient in number and in kind to produce the superb optical system of a gull's eye. So what has been done for over a century and a quarter, with each generation imprinting a mental pattern on the next, is to quit logic by an appeal to belief. Since the gull's eye exists, it must be so – a claim so weak in logic that it has no value worth speaking about. Had you been born with a fortune and spent it improvidently, you would now have little money in your bank account. Right now, it is indeed true that you have little money in your account. Therefore you must have been born with a fortune, and spent it improvidently. The mental process here is just the same as it is in biology. Such inferential conclusions are empty unless it can be proved strictly that the conclusion could be arrived at in no other way: in the analogy, it would be necessary to prove that only by being born with a fortune and subsequently spending it could one arrive at a small bank balance. In biology it has never been proved that the optical system of a gull's eye can be arrived at in no other way except through evolution by natural selection, and in the absence of such an essential proof what is done is to replace proof by an article of faith without which no biologist could secure a job.

With the nineteenth-century theory essentially useless, two alternatives remain: evolution in a comparatively few large steps essentially miraculous in their origin, or evolution in large steps as a result of the arrival on the Earth of genetic systems from outside. Quite apart from the aversion of the scientist to miracles, there are plenty of reasons why importations from outside provide the correct explanation for the evolution of life on the Earth. Returning to the case of the eye, whereas the gull's eye is so near to optical perfection, the eyes possessed by terrestrial creatures are generally very far from performing optimally with respect to the light intensity. Full sunlight, defined, shall we say, by the glare from a snowfield, is far too bright. For humans, dark glasses are obligatory in such conditions. Dark glasses are advisable in any tropical light, even in light which has been poorly reflected with only, say, 10 per cent efficiency from the land surface. The most comfortable light intensity for the human eye lies in the range from one hundredth to one thousandth of full sunlight, which is about the intensity of the artificial lighting in a well-lit office. This is roughly the intensity that would be seen by a person standing on a snowfield on one of the satellites of the planet Uranus. Photosynthesis by plants also works with poor efficiency in full sunlight; it works with maximum efficiency at significantly lower intensities. Interestingly, the lowest intensity of light at which plants can grow turns out to be about the level at which the human eye feels most comfortable. It is natural to think that, since the eye is so perfectly constructed from the standpoint of physical optics, it is probably also well constructed from the point of view of the intensity of the light in the environment in which it evolved. This places the environment in the outer regions of the Solar System, or in some other environment of similar light intensity, the same being true for the complex biochemical processes of photosynthesis.

Some biologists have asked what is to be gained by such a theory, and the answers to this question are several. First, it corresponds better to the facts. Second, the Universe at large is much better fitted to bear the genetic cost of evolution than the Earth alone. And third, most problems of origin turn out to broaden in their horizons until they become cosmological in scope, so it is likely that the problem of life, perhaps the biggest of all problems, is universal in its scale. Scientists often seem to feel that a simple theory is more likely to be correct than a complex one. While simplicity, once we understand the relevant mathematics, does seem to be a property of the basic physical laws, complexity is the hallmark of the applications of those laws. A river flows smoothly in a broad, gently shelving bed and it all looks placid and simple, but let the bed of the river fall suddenly by twenty metres or so, and amazing complexities are instantly let loose at the resulting waterfall. What had been the fairly simple problem of describing the smooth flow of water suddenly becomes essentially insoluble in its details at the drop in the bed of the river. Surely this is the way it goes in all aspects of the Universe, probably the most significant changes taking place in hiatuses, in disasters, in sudden shifts from smooth uneventful conditions. The same appears to be generally true of human society, with governments perpetually trying to maintain conditions of smooth flow, but with the events that really determine history occurring in uncontrollable shifts, as society plunges in its evolution over a series of waterfalls which set all manner of unexpected events in train.

In our view, so it has been for the development of life on Earth. From time to time the Earth has been flooded by immense genetic storms which changed many species drastically and sometimes even extinguished them altogether. The view we have maintained since 1978 is that viruses provide the vehicle of biological change, not the ineffective mis-copying from generation to generation of the usual evolutionary theory. According to the ideas developed in this book, the immediate source of the viruses is the cloud of evaporated cometary material in which the Earth is perpetually embedded, from which the Earth's atmosphere is known to pick up some 1000 tonnes per annum, sufficient in quantity to supply of the order of 10^{21} bacteria and 10^{25} viruses. We have seen that the reason why some comets come to the inner regions of the Solar System, supplying material to the halo around the Earth when they do so, is that from time to time a passing star disturbs the cloud of comets that surrounds the Solar System, and on rarer occasions the Solar System approaches a galactic molecular cloud. The more frequent encounters with passing stars yield a steady supply of comets, but at a rather low rate such as we are experiencing at present. The rare encounters with molecular clouds, occurring only once or twice every 100 million years, yield a much larger influx of comets diverted into the inner regions of the Solar System. For a million years or so, the time for which such a large influx of comets persists, the halo of evaporated material becomes much denser, providing an intense supply of viruses to the Earth and a resulting genetic storm, producing both extinctions and rapid evolution among terrestrial plants and animals.

As far as extinctions go, the worst genetic storm of all seems to have occurred about 65 million years ago, when every species of animal weighing more than 25 kilograms or so became extinct, including the large dinosaurs. The dinosaurs were far from being alone in their fate, which was shared by nearly half the genera of all animals. None of the many proposed physical and chemical causes of these disasters appears to us to be plausible, for the reason that, while nonbiological disasters could conceivably attenuate a species, wholly exterminating a species is unlikely. Physical extermination is very difficult, as is evidenced by the inability of man, with all his technology, to exterminate scarcely a single one of the many millions of insect species. The extinctions of 65 million years ago were not confined to large animals: they went all the way down to microorganisms, and they occurred in every kind of habitat, including the bottom of the sea, showing that whatever the cause was it drenched the whole Earth and reached into every nook and cranny.

It is useful here to set out the geological periods and timescales of relevance to the evolutionary development of terrestrial life, as shown in Figure 14.5. The time of 65 million years ago will be seen to lie near the boundary between the Cretaceous period and the Tertiary, the latter with its subdivisions of Paleocene, Eocene, Oligocene, Miocene and Pliocene.

Figure 14.6 shows the record of the beginnings and endings of a number of genera of small sea-living animals, their period of existence from the beginning of the Cretaceous onwards being shown by the horizontal bars. Plankton are surface creatures, and the benthic

163

relative duration of eras		era	period	epoch	duration in million of years (approx.)	millions of years ago (approx.)
Cenozoic		Cenozoic	Quaternary	Holocene	approx. last 10,000 years	
				Pleistocene	2.5	2.5
Mesozoic			Tertiary	Pliocene	4.5	7
				Miocene	19	26
Paleozoic				Oligocene	12	38
				Eocene	16	54
				Paleocene	11	65
		Mesozoic	Cretaceous		71	136
			Jurassic		54	190
			Triassic		35	225
Precambrian		Paleozoic	Permian		55	280
			Carbon-iferous Pennsylvanian		45	325
			Carbon-iferous Mississippian		20	345
			Devonian		50	395
			Silurian		35	430
			Ordovician		70	500
			Cambrian		70	570
			Precambrian		4,030	
formation of Earth's crust 4,600,000,000 years ago						

Figure 14.5 The geological timescale.

creatures are (or were) from great oceanic depths. Of the 15 cases of extinction, 14 terminate at the Cretaceous/Tertiary boundary, about 65 million years ago. Of the 9 genera which began in post-Jurassic times, 5 started at the Cretaceous/Tertiary boundary, suggesting

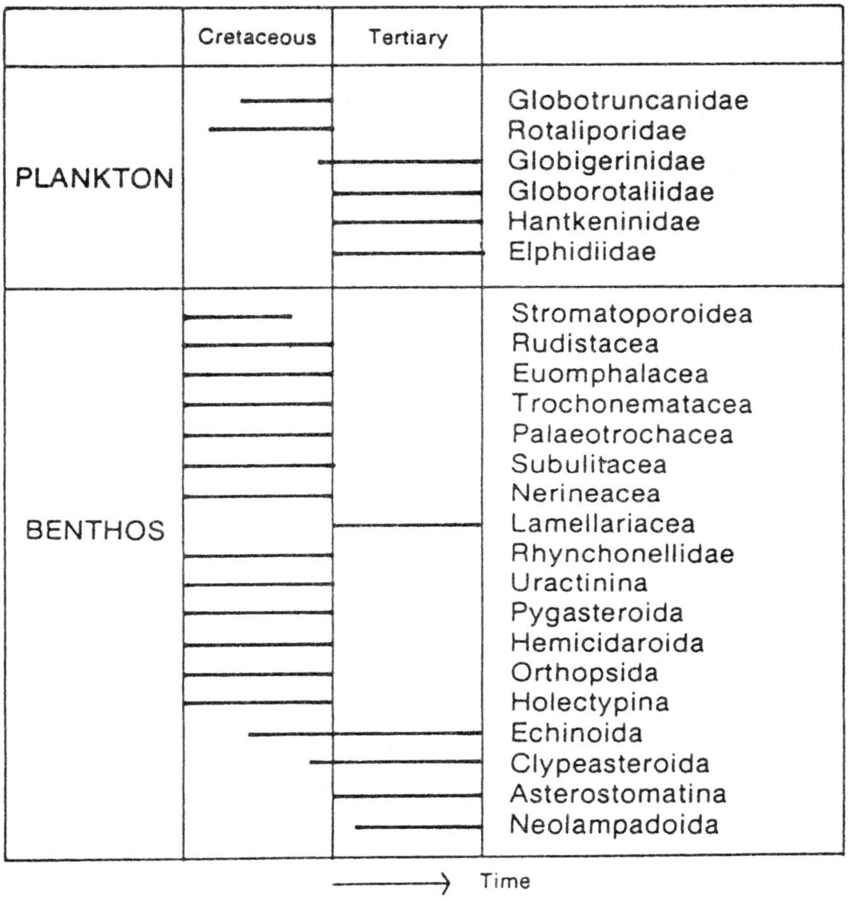

	Cretaceous	Tertiary	
PLANKTON			Globotruncanidae Rotaliporidae Globigerinidae Globorotaliidae Hantkeninidae Elphidiidae
BENTHOS			Stromatoporoidea Rudistacea Euomphalacea Trochonematacea Palaeotrochacea Subulitacea Nerineacea Lamellariacea Rhynchonellidae Uractinina Pygasteroida Hemicidaroida Orthopsida Holectypina Echinoida Clypeasteroida Asterostomatina Neolampadoida

⟶ Time

Figure 14.6 The periods of existence, denoted by horizontal bars, of various genera of small sea-living animals, with plankton from the surface water and benthic creatures from considerable oceanic depths. (After D. A. Russell, in *Syllogeus* No. 12, National Museums of Canada, 1976.)

that the situation 65 million years ago could be a beginning as well as an ending, a necessary condition for understanding the entire process of evolution.

165

CHAPTER FIFTEEN

An attempted synthesis

Bacterial life on the Earth extended back in time to at least 3600 m.y. BP (million years before the present). From the birth of the Earth some 4600 m.y. BP until about 3800 m.y. BP, heavy bombardment by missiles largely of cometary origin obliterated the geological record. Since a bombardment that was sufficient to destroy rocks would surely have annihilated life, 3800 m.y. BP is the first time at which life could have secured a long-lasting hold on the Earth. The comparatively short gap between 3600 m.y. BP, when life had indeed secured such a hold, and the moment at 3800 m.y. BP when heavy bombardment ceased is the first of a number of surprising features of biological history. It is important to realize that this gap of 200 million years could have been shorter – indeed, it could have been nothing at all. Recently geologists have found indirect evidence for life in the Earth's oldest rocks in the form of a subtle enhancement of the heavy isotope of carbon, C-13 relative to C-12. Because the process of photosynthesis tends to concentrate the heavier isotope of carbon to a very slight degree one might argue that photosynthetic microbial life was already thriving on the Earth at 3800 m.y. BP. Thus life exists in the fossil record from the very first moment it was physically possible for it to do so.

Although bacteria are simple life-forms in the sense that they operate on only some 2000 genes compared with the 100,000 or so in complex creatures like ourselves, the 2000 genes each have the immense measure of complexity discussed in Chapter 14. The enzymes to which they give rise catalyse with great efficiency reactions which are central to the chemistry of the carbon atom, and which are also central to creatures like ourselves, for instance the reactions by which energy is extracted from the sugars. Similarities of operation are so great that enzymes from a bacterium can function very well in the cells of a man. Hence, by as early as 3600 m.y. BP possibly as early as 3800 m.y. BP, many of the biological problems of crucial consequence to all life had been solved. If life originated earlier than this in the Universe at large, there is of course no difficulty in seeing how the biochemical complexities of life could have been imported onto the Earth from the moment the Earth could first sustain life. But if one attempts to follow orthodox biology, according to which life originated here on Earth, the severe problem arises of how to explain the origin in a narrow window situated near 3800 m.y. BP. The miracles of choice discussed in the preceding chapter are required to have happened then, in a thin slice of geological history; if heat within rocks between 3800 and 3600 m.y. old had not destroyed the morphological fossil evidence, it might very well be a slice with no thickness at all, an imaginary slice that never existed. Those who support the orthodox view have made no worthwhile progress in clarifying this situation. Faced with the super-astronomical numbers of Chapter 14, we would hardly expect them to succeed.

There is a clear distinction between the relatively simple bacterial cells (prokaryotes) with their 2000 genes and the much more complex cells of eukaryotes with more genes and larger sizes, of which baker's yeast is an example, or the cells of algae growing on a pond. The diameter of bacterial cells is typically about 1 micrometre, that of eukaryotic cells typically 10 micrometres: a thousandfold difference in volume. In this greater volume, eukaryotes contain not only the basic DNA with its double helix but also many attendant structures, each of which themselves have the aspects of a prokaryotic cell. It is generally thought that the first eukaryotic cells appeared on the Earth between 1500 and 2000 m.y. BP, although there are a few paleontologists who set the date of their appearance appreciably earlier than this. At any rate, by 1000 m.y. BP the Earth was widely populated both by prokaryotes and by single-celled eukaryotes like algae. Here we already have a distinction between primary producers (plants) and predators (animals).

To help understand the difference between the two, it is worth noticing that the foundation of all life lies in a remarkable chemical coincidence, namely that the energy of attachment of the two oxygen atoms to carbon in the carbon dioxide molecule is almost exactly the same as that of the four hydrogen atoms to carbon in the methane molecule. This permits carbon to oscillate in its allegiance to oxygen and hydrogen according to the reversible chemical reaction

$$CO_2 + 4H_2 \rightleftharpoons CH_4 + 2H_2O$$

(the symbol $\rightleftharpoons$ indicating that the reaction can proceed in either direction according to prevailing conditions). At low temperatures the reaction proceeds from left to right, and enzymes encourage it to go in that direction. A whole kingdom of bacteria is predicated on this, bacteria whose activities, we think, are responsible for the quantities of methane observed in the atmospheres of the planets Jupiter, Saturn, Uranus and Neptune. The suggestion by Professor T. Gold (*Power from the Earth*, J. M. Dent, 1987) that carbonaceous material first arrived on the Earth in a hydrated form also derives plausibility from the same process, and indeed the observed presence of hydrocarbons in comets, observations made largely since 1986, have proved it beyond reasonable doubt. The point is important when taken together with Gold's contention that the subsequent oxidation of terrestrial hydrocarbons, a process taking place within the Earth at a depth of 100 kilometres or more, plays a primary role in the genesis of a wide range of terrestrial phenomena – earthquakes, volcanoes and possibly the larger-scale movements described now-adays in terms of plate tectonics.

A more complex chemical picture, but again dependent on the nearly equal allegiance of carbon to oxygen and to hydrogen, is a controlling factor both for a second kingdom of bacteria and for eukaryotic organisms. Writing only the inputs and outputs from whole arrays of chemical reactions, the reactions in question are

168

$$5CO_2 + 5H_2O \rightleftharpoons C_5H_{10}O_5 + 5O_2,$$

$$6CO_2 + 6H_2O \rightleftharpoons C_6H_{12}O_6 + 6O_2,$$

with $C_5H_{10}O_5$ and $C_6H_{12}O_6$ accounting (with the various structural arrangements of atoms these basic formulas represent) for most of the sugars, the energy sources of the more complex forms of life. Enzymes help these reactions to proceed in the right-to-left direction, no other stimulus being necessary; but to make them go from left to right an external stimulus is required. The external stimulus is sunlight, the reactions from left to right being commonly referred to as photosynthesis. Joining sugar molecules together in various ways gives carbohydrates like starch and cellulose, and also the substance forming the shells of shrimps and lobsters, fingernails and the beaks of birds. And the O_2 on the right-hand sides of the reactions is the oxygen in the air that we breathe. All this is derived from the three commonest elements in the Universe (helium apart).

So, we have looked at three kingdoms of organisms: a kingdom of methane-producing bacteria, a kingdom of photosynthetic bacteria and a kingdom of eukaryotic organisms of which algae are an example. Photosynthetic bacteria differ from eukaryotic organisms in one subtle and (it seems to us) highly significant feature. Instead of water, photosynthetic bacteria rely on reactions involving hydrogen sulphide:

$$5CO_2 + 10H_2S \rightarrow C_5H_{10}O_5 + 5H_2O + 10S.$$

On the Earth water is exceedingly common, while H_2S is rare, being largely confined to effluents from volcanoes. So here is another awkward problem for those who believe in an Earth-centred origin of life. Why use what is rare rather than what is common? The implication is that photosynthetic bacteria developed in other places where H_2S was not so rare. Perhaps the other places were colder than the Earth, where the freezing point of H_2S (minus 85°C rather than 0°C) could have been a relevant factor.

Provided there are organisms around that exploit the left-to-right, photosynthetic reactions, it is possible for other organisms to dispense with them. These other organisms are predators that obtain their sugars (essential for these reactions to proceed in the opposite energy-producing direction) from the photosynthetic organisms. This eating of photosynthetic organisms had the advantage of dispensing with the complex chemistry needed to support the left-to-right reactions, thereby lightening the genetic load on the other organisms and permitting them to develop other remarkable properties – for instance the property of locomotion. These other organisms are what we call animals. Taxonomists accord to animals a kingdom in their own right, making a present-day total of four taxonomic kingdoms. By 1000 m.y. BP the four kingdoms were all established on the Earth. But as yet they were all kingdoms of single-celled organisms.

The first multicelled organisms are found in the fossil record at about 700 m.y. BP. But the haul is thin compared to the immense proliferation of such organisms that occurred 570 m.y. BP. It was the discovery of this proliferation by geologists that was taken long ago to mark a crucial separation in the record, that between the Precambrian and the Cambrian, a separation shown clearly in Figure 14.5. The new creatures were animals, referred to collectively as the metazoans. Until recently the metazoans of 700 m.y. BP were taken to be the precursors of the explosion 570 m.y. BP, but in a recent book Professor Stephen Jay Gould assures us that this was not so (*Wonderful Life*, Penguin, 1989). The new conclusions come from careful studies of exceedingly well-preserved fossils found in the Burgess Shale, a layer of rock formed from deposits laid down during the Cambrian period. Well over a hundred species have been identified, many with details of internal structures. It would seem that the fossilization conditions were exceptional in protecting the dead bodies from scavengers and bacteria and from contact with oxygen. Compressed in fine silt, the bodies were preserved as films of carbon on the slaty bedding planes of the shale that eventually came to be formed. Formerly, paleontological information about the structures of the early metazoans was confined to surviving hard parts of their bodies, but from 1970 onwards, thanks largely to the techniques developed by Professor H. B. Whittington and his colleagues at Cambridge University, it became possible to arrive at more extensive judgements on the basis of studying the carbonized soft body parts. By using improved techniques to study these remains, it became clear that the metazoans of 570 m.y. BP were not derived from those of 700 m.y. BP; the latter appear either to have died out or to have been overwhelmed in the later explosion.

Just as 3800 m.y. BP being when life first appears in the record poses a severe problem for Earth-centred Darwinists, so does the flood of metazoan life at 570 m.y. BP. Where is its previous evolutionary history and why did it suddenly happen when it did? It is indicative of the paucity of ideas from the pre-Copernican biological establishment that, whereas Professor Gould's entertaining and informative book contains 323 pages, only five (pp. 228–32) are given over to these crucial questions.

The post-Copernican outlook developed in the present book finds no difficulty in explaining what happened at the Precambrian boundary. Its motion around the galaxy took the Solar System close to a molecular cloud. Cometary orbits in the Oort Cloud at large distances from the Sun were considerably perturbed, and many comets acquired new orbits of a highly elongated form which brought them into the inner regions of the Solar System. Among the incoming comets was a swarm of smaller bodies, some of which intersected the Earth's orbit exactly and at the same time, showering down onto the Earth a rain of meteoritic bodies. Just as the interiors of the meteorites that fall today can remain cool, so it was with members of the great swarm that fell 570 m.y. BP. A fraction contained not just bacteria and viruses, but also the frozen eggs of metazoan creatures. It would not be unreasonable to suppose that simple metazoan life forms developed and flourished within huge aqueous lakes in billions of very large comets. Such objects would have eventually refrozen and fragmented into a multitude of smaller cometary bodies. The metazoan explosion thus came from a swarm of such bodies falling onto the Earth, so that no long evolutionary period on the Earth was required and no explicit precursors were needed. While there may very well have been extensive evolution to produce the metazoans, just as there must have been extensive evolution to produce bacteria, the evolution was not on the Earth.

But the question remains of why it took so long, from 3800 to 570 m.y. BP, for this to happen. As we remarked earlier, the timescale for the approach of the Solar System to a molecular cloud should be about 100 m.y., not over 1000 m.y. The time of rotation of our galaxy is about 250 m.y., and it is this that determines the time frame for all such problems. There is good paleontological evidence to support this view. As well as the explosive biological outburst marking the end of the long Precambrian period, there have since been two major events which appear to be associated with cometary swarms, a blizzard of extinctions in the Permian at about 250 m.y. BP and the widely-discussed extinctions (especially of dinosaurs) at the end of the Cretaceous, 65 m.y. BP. The three episodes, probably associated with cometary swarms, at 570, 250 and 65 m.y. BP have an average spacing close to 250 m.y., close to the orbital period of the Solar System in the galaxy, an association that has been remarked upon by Victor Clube, among others. Hence between 3600 and 570 m.y. BP there should have been upwards of ten major incursions into the inner Solar System by cometary swarms. One such swarm appears to have done something which shows in the fossil record at 700 m.y. BP, or possibly somewhat earlier, but why did nothing major happen over the vast interval from 3600 to 1000 m.y. BP? We continue by offering an answer which, although speculative, at least has the merit of being interesting.

For them to survive, the metazoan eggs needed to fall into water, not on land, and the water had to be shallow, not more than a hundred metres or so deep. There is shallow water on the present Earth, the considerable shelf on the eastern side of North America, the European continental shelf and an extensive shallow sea stretching from Malaysia to northern Australia. But for the rest there is not very much. The western margin of North America drops steeply into the Pacific. River deltas apart, there is not much anywhere in South America, nor down the coast of West Africa. But what if, up to about 1000 m.y. BP, the crustal movements which have generated the modern topography were absent? What if, almost everywhere, the continental margins fell steeply to the ocean floor, as they still do in so many places today? Then the probability of a successful landing for metazoans would be appreciably reduced, perhaps to the point where not even ten or more major episodes of cometary bombardment were sufficient to establish them on the Earth.

But we can still question why it has been different during the last

1000 m.y. Reference was made earlier to Gold's idea that it has been the oxidation of buried hydrocarbons that generates tectonic activities such as earthquakes, volcanoes and perhaps crustal movements. The oxygen involved comes from rock, the reactions in question being considerably temperature dependent. It is only when the temperature is high, 1000°C or more, that anything significant in this respect may be expected to happen. The source of the heat is probably radioactivity, the heat from which remains trapped in the lower rocks for thousands of millions of years, with temperatures rising slowly as more and more radioactive heat is released. Some radioactive substances release their heat comparatively quickly (on the geological timescale), but the greatest contributions come from those with long lifetimes, explicitly from the heavier isotope of uranium, uranium-238, with a half-life of 4500 m.y. and an isotope of thorium, thorium-232, with a half-life of 14000 m.y. Thus it would be necessary to wait pretty much the whole lifetime of the Earth for the major contributions to radioactive heating to become available. According to Gold, this would lead to faster oxidation of hydrocarbons and to more Earth activity generally. Perhaps it was this that eventually led to the Earth being provided with an adequate landing space for metazoan life to establish itself on our planet.

No primary trunk for the tree of life has been found. The four kingdoms of terrestrial organisms, two bacterial, two eukaryotic (vegetable and animal), have no discernible common ancestor, either in the fossil record or in the genetic material of representatives of the four kingdoms. This is yet another blow to Earth-centred Darwinists, who postulate a primary trunk to their tree but cannot find it, another blow to add to all the others that rain down on their heads, a rain which will increase relentlessly in its intensity until their position eventually disintegrates. This is the way the Universe ultimately has its say, ultimately forcing a correct point of view to be adopted. We humans do not really invent or discover what is correct in science; rather, the Universe eventually torments us into it.

If indeed there really is a tree of life, kingdoms are at best the primary branches, phyla are secondary branches, classes are tertiary branches, orders are fourth-order branches, families are fifth, genera sixth and species seventh. It is possible to entertain a measure of cynicism about biological taxonomy, for classification is the method to which scientists invariably turn whenever they do not understand a phenomenon. All systems of classification start from a set of defined units, species in the biological case. For species that are presently living, the specification of units is well marked and acceptable. To these in biology is added what are decided by taxonomists and paleontologists to be species in the fossil record. Over this addition there has often been argument and disagreement. Setting any such issues aside, suppose the initial set of units is well and truly specified. The units being far from identical, as different kinds of star are far from identical, some are more similar to each other than to the rest. The properties by which similarities are to be judged must next be precisely stated and a list of them drawn up. Properly speaking, the list should be drawn up, agreed on and never changed thereafter. Experience of watching classificationists at work shows them to be perpetually chopping and changing their list. Once a classification has become widely accepted, the chopping and changing largely stops. Later, in retrospect it might seem as if everything had fallen neatly and naturally into place right from the start, but this is rarely so.

Leaving aside this first reason for entertaining a measure of cynicism, each property on the list has to be sharp in the sense that a unit either possesses it or does not. Thus, for each property we can divide the ensemble of units into those with the property and those without it. Those with the property form a subset of the whole ensemble, and those without the property form the complementary subset. A prominent example in biology would be any property which distinguished plants from animals. There are many such properties, and where it happens that many properties all define the same subset, the division thus achieved is regarded as especially significant. The properties in question are then grouped together in our list into accepted criteria for establishing a division of the ensemble (in the above example, all the criteria that distinguish plants from animals). The next step is to look for a nesting of subsets, one completely inside another. When this happens the units of the nested subset possess all the properties that distinguished the larger subset, together with additional properties of their own, the latter being common to the units of the smaller subset and not possessed by any other unit in the whole ensemble. If all the properties distinguishing the units happen to form a coherent system of nested subsets, the classification can be said to be complete and successful. The ensemble is divided first into large subsets, of which there may only be two, as with plants and animals, then each subset is divided into secondary subsets, then tertiary subsets, and so on, a hierarchical arrangement to which the analogy of the branching tree can be applied.

But what if we do not arrive at a coherent system of nested subsets? What if subsets sometimes cross the boundaries of other subsets? There are two things we can then do. One is to drop the whole idea and wait until we have a better understanding of the matter; the other is to play around with the list of properties used to classify the ensemble. We can ask whether there is any way that we can adjust the list so as to arrive at a coherent system of nested subsets. Should the answer be affirmative, the more difficult question then arises of whether the eventual success is no more than a subjective effect of our own choices, or whether the eventual success continues to have a valid scientific significance. This question almost surely has to be asked about the whole system of biological taxonomy. Biologists have for more than a century answered the questions positively. The positive answer came with Darwinism, and ever since it has over-whelmed the scientific world like a tidal wave. The judgement may be correct, but the unbiased observer of the biological scene will also see the justification for the measures of cynicism we mentioned above.

It has been remarked that the primary trunk of the tree of life is not to be found here on Earth. Accepting biological taxonomy at face value, the first evidence of life on Earth is of four branches, the four kingdoms discussed above. What, then, were the metazoans that appeared at the Precambrian boundary? Textbooks on biological taxonomy refer to them as a subkingdom, neither a primary branch nor a secondary branch but something in between. This is the way it always goes when classifications are empirically based, on procedure rather than knowledge. Classificationists no sooner think they have a neatly specified system than cases come along which cannot be fitted in, and for which subclasses have to be invented. This happens because classificationists are in some respects like children forcing together the pieces of a jigsaw puzzle: the eventual picture is never quite right, and the discrepancies show up in the need to invent subdivisions. In the days before physicists understood the nature of light, considerable importance was attached to the division of visible light into the seven colours of the rainbow. If financial support had been available and if transport had been sufficiently rapid, one can imagine physicists in those days travelling to world conferences to discuss what it was that separated the colours one from another, an issue seen to be irrelevant once the nature of light became understood. One can imagine acrimonious arguments taking place over the irrelevant issue of whether a particular ray of light belonged to orange light or to green, and one can suspect that empirical classifications always work themselves into this kind of unprofitable cul-de-sac.

But to proceed with the metazoans! The first step in classifying metazoans is into secondary branches, phyla. The properties defining a phylum may be described with a fair approximation as the properties that determine body plan. All organisms in the same phylum are built on the same body plan. Repeatedly in *Wonderful Life*, Professor Gould expresses profound wonder that the number of distinctive body plans which emerged in the great outburst at 570 m.y. BP was significantly larger than the number existing today. From this he arrives at the conclusion that former ideas about biological evolution were upside down. Instead of life evolving since 570 m.y. BP towards ever-increasing complexity, it has proceeded via a cutting down of possibilities, by restriction rather than by diversity. This raises issues that may very well be profound, and which we now discuss by way of concluding our book.

In the first place, the greater number of phyla at 570 m.y. BP does not seem to us as significant as Professor Gould would have it. The definition of what constitutes a phylum is not entirely clear-cut. Professor Gould mentions that some taxonomists count as few as 20 phyla among presently existing species, whereas others count as many as 32. The *Encyclopaedia Britannica* gives 28, which we shall assume to be correct in the present discussion. The extra phyla present at 530 m.y. BP, and thought to be present back as far as 570 m.y. BP, number 8 in the table given on pp. 209–10 of *Wonderful Life*. Additionally, there are 13 cases of a unique organism. If each of these is accorded a new phylum to itself, the total of phyla distinct from modern phyla is 21. Accepting that all modern phyla were also present at 570 m.y. BP gives a total then of 49, of which 28 have survived.

According to our point of view, what arrives from space will always have a wider genetic range than what survives on the Earth, simply because the Universe is a far broader habitat than the Earth. It is just for this reason that bacteria have so many unearthly properties. Viruses may also be expected to have a wider spectrum than those which attack the cells of terrestrial organisms. And the incoming eggs of metazoans would be expected to include many varieties that did not succeed in eventually establishing themselves on the Earth. Landing on a new planet must entail significant losses. It would indeed be embarrassing to our point of view if the situation were otherwise.

We can agree with Professor Gould that what constitutes complexity in an animal is a matter of judgement. It is quite likely that if complexity is based on bodily structure and on the subtleties of mechanical motion, then a shrimp is as complex as a man. But there is an important sense in which animals since 570 m.y. BP have been evolving towards increasing complexity – the electronic sense. The ability of animals to store data, to process it, and to act on the processed information has undoubtedly increased more or less steadily over the geological period from the Cambrian onwards. Professor Gould accepts human consciousness as an exception to his general thesis; it is a phenomenon sudden in its appearance and exceptional in its nature. Again, we have to doubt that this was so. In our opinion, consciousness grows with electronic complexity. We think that all of what are called the higher animals possess it in some degree. What other animals do not possess is the linguistic ability to tell us how they feel. But it needs no great powers of inference to deduce the presence of consciousness from the way they behave.

The recent work on the soft-bodied life-forms from 530 m.y. BP of fossils found in the Burgess Shale of a quarry in the Yoho Canadian National Park, and fossils from nearby deposits dating back to 570 m.y. BP, does not go against the arguments given in earlier chapters. Nor does it not preclude later landings of metazoans at post-Cambrian dates. This is provided the phyla present in later landings did not go outside the range of those which arrived at 570 m.y. BP. The earlier arrivals could largely have become extinct, some being renewed in the later landings and others, such as the trilobites, not. On the other hand, it is also possible that the great event of 570 m.y. BP did indeed provide the starting point of all the present-day phyla of animals. It is possible that all of metazoan evolution since 570 m.y. BP has consisted simply in making genetic grafts onto the various stocks which that great event had supplied. However, we still need the grafting to have occurred in sudden major bursts in order to explain why essentially all the important transitions are not seen in the fossil record. The explanation given previously in terms of viral invasions still holds, but with the possibility that an interesting change can be made in one important respect.

We have seen that there is an overwhelming case against the neo-Darwinian concept of new genes being developed from the outset by random internal changes within organisms. The immense super-astronomical numbers in Chapter 14 demonstrate this critical point beyond doubt. It was for this reason that we had to postulate the arrival of new genes grafted through viruses onto older stocks at each of the major evolutionary shifts. But now it can be seen that there is an alternative to this hypothesis. The new genes *could be there already*, within the creatures which arrived at 570 m.y. BP. They could lie dormant, unexpressed, until triggered into activity by viruses in the same kind of invasions as discussed before. This makes the viruses act only as switches, not both as switches and as the suppliers of new genes. Viruses certainly do act as switches, changing the operation of cell programs in decisive ways. This is a matter of fact, whereas the idea of viruses also supplying new genes was a matter of hypothesis which we are free to change, if an alternative hypothesis should seem more promising.

On the subject of hypotheses, Professor Thomas Gold has said that 'in the matter of framing hypotheses it does not pay to be trivial'. To this we would add an aphorism of our own: 'Provided a hypothesis is not contradicted by any certain fact, the more startling its consequences the more likely it is to be true.' In this spirit we end by briefly examining the consequences of the hypothesis that all the genes necessary for the development of animal life were already present in the creatures which arrived on the Earth in great profusion at 570 m.y. BP. This hypothesis is surely startling enough, for it implies that the genes that would eventually, 570 m.y. later, provide for the intellectual emergence of man – a mysterious phenomenon as the quotation from Alfred Russel Wallace given in Chapter 5 made abundantly clear – were already present but unexpressed in the creatures which inhabited the shallow seas of Cambrian times. The situation was analogous to the larval state of insects, with the creatures operating initially on a comparatively simple genetic program but with much more complex genetic information held in reserve.

It is now that viruses enter the story. To use an analogy from computing, a virus may be thought of as changing a number of addresses in transfer instructions within the controlling section of a program. In the description of the operation of a virus quoted from Sir Christopher Andrewes at the beginning of Chapter 11, the virus succeeded in setting up a closed loop which served to replicate itself. These are the readily observable cases. There must be many others, one might think, where a virus does not succeed as smoothly as in Sir Christopher's description, where a virus only manages to change a cell program in a more or less disordered way. Occasionally, among the creatures which multiplied to produce many billions of members in the wake of the great event of 570 m.y. BP, the disordering would lead to as yet unexpressed genes being addressed. The process is not controlled in a detailed and systematic way. While it may have some degree of control, the random element in it means that most creatures would not survive. Even whole phyla might not survive, as happened to the trilobites. But among the immense swarm of possibilities, some creatures survived. Some phyla may indeed have been proof against viral invasion, and they remained as they were. Continuing in their resistance to viral invasion they survived to the present day, as the so-called living fossils. But the fraction that were infected and survived were left in a strange, distorted condition no longer well adapted to their environment. We can imagine the survivors struggling in a bemused condition in search of other means of existence, other means different from that of their ancestors.

The emergence of amphibians from the sea to intertidal regions and thence onto the land is often represented in adventurous language. We would rather see this as a desperate, even random move by bemused and disoriented creatures. The creatures worked with extreme inefficiency, because over the 100 million or so generations that had elapsed since 570 m.y. BP the new genes that were now compelled to operate were in a seriously garbled condition, about one base pair in ten on their DNA having been garbled by mis-copying. This meant that the catalytic property of the proteins which the garbled new genes produced were weaker than they would have been for pristine genes. The reason for the garbling was that the new genes had not been protected over some 100 million generations by natural selection, because the genes in question were not being actively used over those many generations. They had suffered from mis-copying without having incurred any selective penalty.

But the woefully inefficient creatures that stumbled into an amphibious environment had one crucial advantage: there were no predators in their new environment to trouble them, no birds in the air to snap them up as they emerged from the sea. Some survived and managed precariously to replicate, and it was then that a bio-logical miracle occurred, a miracle that is not possible in any other evolutionary scenario we have encountered, a miracle so striking from a genetic point of view that it gives us a strong feeling that the present scenario must be substantially correct. Although the garbling in every individual of one base pair in ten makes a sad inefficient creature of every individual, the ensemble of surviving creatures taken as a whole still contains all the original genetic information of the new genes when in their pristine form. This is because the base pairs garbled in one individual are not the same as those garbled in another. Taken collectively, the correct genetic messages still outnumber incor-rect messages by a ratio of about ten to one. It is now that the system of crossover in sexual reproduction really comes to its own in a way it never does in orthodox genetics. For each breeding couple of genetically distinct members from the ensemble, offspring will be widely variable in the fraction of base pairs that are garbled, and in a limited population those with less garbling are the ones which survive into the next generation. Because half of the genetic material that is discarded at each generation will be heavily weighted with respect to the disoriented base pairs, in only a few tens of generations (or at most a few hundred) the original genes will be recovered in essentially their pristine form. In a flash, on an evolutionary timescale, the fully functioning genes will be recovered and a new creature will have become established, established at the expense of all those former species which did not manage to survive the transition. This scenario corresponds so well to the explosive rapidity of the great steps in biological evolution, rapid quite beyond what can be captured in the fossil record, that we have come to believe it must contain the essential features of the process of biological evolution, the outstanding feature being that genes necessary for progress up the evolutionary ladder must exist beforehand – just the point that puzzled Alfred Russel Wallace.

It is an obvious corollary that a great deal of work still needs to be done in order to understand evolution in the Universe at large. So far as the Earth is concerned the picture is in a sense creationary, the creation for metazoans occurring at 570 m.y. BP. The input then, in the form of the architecture of living structures – plants and animals, was closely equivalent to the output, the overall process by which the input was converted into the present-day output being pretty much the one outlined by the science of paleontology. This is not an explanation in any very deep way of the ultimate origin and evolution of life, such as orthodox biology dubiously claims to provide. Rather it is a debunking of those claims which form an impediment to gaining any real understanding of the nature of life and of its cosmic heritage; it is a doorway leading to a different landscape which it will be the privilege of the next generation, or generations, to explore.

It has been emphasized throughout this book that nonscientific constraints have often stood in the way of exploring new conceptual landscapes. The first phase of the Copernican Revolution, recounted in Chapter 2, showed clearly the difficulty of getting even simple facts accepted when they ran counter to religious belief. Science as we know it was of course nurtured mainly within Judaeo-Christian cultures, and so it was only natural that these religions played a decisive role in the past. What turned out unfortunately for science, however, was that the Judaeo-Christian world-view was both human-centred and Earth-centred. The eventual accommodation of a helio-centric system and, later, of Darwin's views were uneasy compromises to say the least, and further extensions of the Copernican Revolution are likely to be resisted with similar vigour. Even in the largely agnostic societies of modern times, ancient religious taboos appear to be deeply ingrained.

Science in the modern world is no longer a monopoly of Christendom, however. We are seeing the rapid emergence of scientific and technological cultures that have distinctly non-Christian roots, as for instance in Japan and the Far East. As these new cultures expand and grow in influence, one might wonder what their effect will be. It is worth noting that Buddhism, which is an important cultural influence in Japan, maintains a refreshingly open attitude and is relatively free from dogma. Gautama Buddha stressed the importance of discovering truth for oneself. On his death-bed, he instructed his disciples thus: 'You should live as lamps unto yourselves. Hold fast to the lamp of Truth. Take refuge only in Truth. Look not to refuge to anyone beside yourself. . . . And those who now in my time or afterwards live thus, they will reach greatness if they are desirous of knowledge' (*Mahaparinibbana Sutra* No. 16). This is exemplary advice to a prospective young scientist, even in the present day. Buddha's own vision of the world was also remarkably post-Copernican, even in the 6th century BC. He describes a Universe composed of billions of 'Minor World Systems', each of which resembles our own planetary system. In the oldest Buddhist texts, which are in effect dialogues of the Buddha, it is stated that in the infinite space of the Universe there exist 'billions of suns, billions of moons . . . billions of Jambudipas, billions of Aparagoyanas, billions of Uttarakurus, billions of Pubbavidehas . . .'. Jambudipas and the other names are words to describe the inhabited regions of the Earth as known to the peoples of northern India at the time. Throughout the dialogues it is amply clear that Buddha viewed life and consciousness (which he thought to be associated with all life) as cosmic phenomena, linked inextricably with the structure of the Universe as a whole.

We thus see that in many important respects the ancient traditions of Buddhism are well suited for extending the Copernican Revolution in the directions we have discussed in this book. If such traditions eventually prevail, science may at last come to be freed of its medieval fetters.

INDEX